CHINESE KITES

CHINESE KITES

An Illustrated Step-by-Step Guide

By Liu Bin

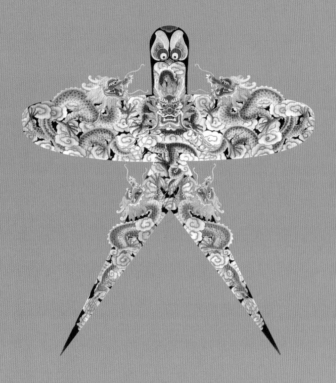

Better Link Press

On page 1
FIG. 1   *Swallow Train* by Liu Bin
Kite train
Swallow kites are some of the most distinctly Chinese kites. They have the swallow as their theme, which is personified through artistic treatment. In the illustration four swallow kites are strung together to form a train.

Above on page 2
FIG. 2   *Eagle* by Zhi Ruili
Soft-wing kite
This kite vividly mimicking an eagle highlights the raptor's powerful build and the impressive width of its wing spread.

Below on page 2
FIG. 3   *Wild Goose* by Zhi Ruili
Soft-wing kite
Unlike the wild geese occurring in nature, which are generally black or gray in color, the wild goose on this kite is painted and decorated in color and exhibits a unique charm.

On page 3
FIG. 4   *Five Dragons* by Liu Bin
Hard-wing kite
This swallow kite has five dragons in different colors as its motif.

Below
FIG. 5   *"Happy Flower Pattern" Dragonfly* by Liu Bin
Soft-wing kite
The drawing on this kite mimics a dragonfly occurring in nature. On a mainly green background, "happy flower patterns" are added in as ornaments. The main motif of the "happy flower pattern" is lotus flowers, full-bodied, dazzling and neatly arranged, a symbol of good luck and fulfilment and happiness. The color contrast between green and pink makes the theme of the kite stand out.

On page 5
FIG. 6   *Turnip* by Liu Bin
Hard-wing kite
This kite takes the shape of a turnip, which is readily recognizable.

Copyright © 2015 Shanghai Press and Publishing Development Company

This book is edited and designed by the Editorial Committee of *Cultural China* series

Diagrams by Liu Bin
Text by Shi Xifa, Liu Bin
Photographs by Liu Bin, Shi Xifa

Translation by Yawtsong Lee
Cover Design by Wang Wei
Interior Design by Li Jing, Hu Bin (Yuan Yinchang Design Studio)

Editors: Wu Yuezhou, Yang Xiaohe
Editorial Director: Zhang Yicong

Senior Consultants: Sun Yong, Wu Ying, Yang Xinci
Managing Director and Publisher: Wang Youbu

ISBN: 978-1-60220-014-2

Address any comments about *Chinese Kites: An Illustrated Step-by-Step Guide* to:

Better Link Press
99 Park Ave
New York, NY 10016
USA

or

Shanghai Press and Publishing Development Company
F 7 Donghu Road, Shanghai, China (200031)
Email: comments_betterlinkpress@hotmail.com

Printed in China by Shenzhen Donnelley Printing Co., Ltd.

1 3 5 7 9 10 8 6 4 2

Contents

FIG. 7   *Soaring Cicada and Bat (Chan Fu Qi Tian)* by Liu Bin
Hard-wing kite
This swallow kite has a cicada body with two pairs of cicada wings. The larger pair of cicada wings on the swallow wings is green and the smaller pair in red is superimposed on the larger pair and extends beyond the swallow wings. Red bat patterns are painted on the wing tips and the waist section. Cicada (*chan*) suggests an endless succession (*chan lian*), while bat (*fu*) portends good fortune (*fu*); this kite therefore represents soaring good fortune in perpetuity.

Contents

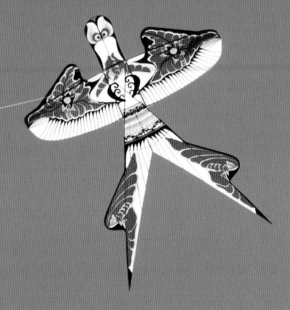

FIG. 8   *Three Abundances and Nine Granted Wishes (San Duo Jiu Ru)* by Liu Bin
Hard-wing kite
This is a swallow kite with auspicious patterns. "Three abundances" (*san duo*)
is represented by a Buddha's Hand citron (*fo shou*), which suggests abundant
fortune (*fu*), a peach, which suggests longevity (*shou*) and a pomegranate,
which, with its many seeds, foretells "plentiful progeny". The kite is also
painted with nine *ruyi* (granted wishes) scepters, representing good wishes.

FOREWORD

I t's a pleasure and a privilege to write a foreword for Liu Bin's new book *Chinese Kites*, which explores various aspects and dimensions of the art of Chinese kites and takes the reader across time and space to a fun part of Chinese culture.

With a rich array of materials and wonderful illustrations, the book fills a gap in the study of the art of Chinese kite-making and helps dispel certain stereotypical views of Chinese kites. The reader who still considers kites to be merely "flying toys" will be disabuses of that notion by this book and be introduced to a whole new vista.

With the unique perspective of a master kite-maker, Liu Bin presents in his book a comprehensive exposé of Chinese kites, giving down-to-earth advice on the selection of kite-making materials as well as sharing original design ideas. With an aesthetic eye inspired by Chinese and Western fine arts, the author gives a detailed account of the art of kite-making with text and image and brings to the fore the cultural and artistic beauty of Chinese kites. The book covers the concepts, aesthetics and categories of Chinese kites, a step-by-step guide to kite-making and the techniques of kite flying. In an easily accessible language, it offers an in-depth look at a fabulous aspect of traditional Chinese culture.

It is my hope that *Chinese Kites* will ignite in the reader a passion for kite-making and flying.

Kong Lingmin
Keeper of the Cao Xueqin tradition of kite-making
(a national-level intangible cultural heritage of China)

Above
FIG. 9 *Blue Goldfish* by Liu Bin
Hard-wing kite
The blue color make this kite very unique and elegant.

Left
FIG. 10 *Buddhism, Taoism and Confucianism* by Kong Lingmin
Paddle kite
The image on this kite is taken from a famous Chinese painting *Picture of Harmony*, signifying the harmonious coexistence of Buddhism, Taoism and Confucianism, and by extension, general harmony.

FIG. 11 *Black Pot Bottom Kite Train* by Liu Bin
Kite train
A train of "black pot bottom" swallow kites in
the blue sky

PREFACE
KITES AND I

Kites and I go back a long way. From the day I was born I have always had kites for company. It is fair to say that kites have witnessed my growing up, my journey into adulthood and my life and career development.

Research and manufacture of kites date back four generations in my family.

First generation: my paternal great grandfather Liu Changfa (1876–1938) was a craftsman in the paper effigies division of the Workshop of the Qing dynasty imperial household in charge of the manufacture of lanterns, fans and kites. He had a special love for kites and mastered the kite-making skills passed down through the ages in the imperial palace. In the turbulent years following the decline of the Qing dynasty (1644–1911), kite-flying lost its popular appeal and, to eke out a living, my great grandfather opened a dumpling shop in Tongxian county of Beijing; at the approach of spring he would make kites to sell. It is much to be regretted that in those years when China was torn by internal strife and foreign invasions, it was not possible to preserve the bulk of his records about kites and the kites themselves.

FIG. 12 In 1982, my grandfather Liu Huiren flew a "dragon kite train" on Tian'anmen Square.

Second generation: my paternal grandfather Liu Huiren (1915–2006) started at the age of 10 to learn systematically from his father the art of kite-making practiced at the imperial court. In my grandfather's time, it was impossible to subsist on kite-making alone and he had to practice a trade unrelated to kites until his retirement. Despite the need to work hard for a living, my grandfather never stopped his exploration and research in the art of kite-making (FIG. 12). Regrettably, many of the drafts, drawings, samples and records in his possession have not been preserved due to their destruction during the "Cultural Revolution".

Third generation: my father Liu Xuejun (1948–), my grandfather's sixth child, lived with his father until the latter's passing. My father, resourceful of mind and skillful with his hands since a child, was passionate about kite-making and proved a quick study. He inherited the family's kite-making tradition and created, together with my grandfather, many of the signature works representing that family tradition.

Fourth generation: born in 1977, I have an unusual knack and flair for designing and crafting kites. Since a child, I have been fascinated by the way my grandfather

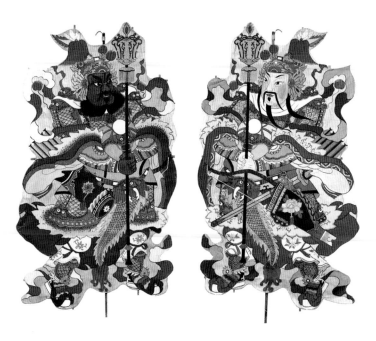

FIG. 13 *Door Gods* by Liu Bin
Paddle kite
In old times people had the custom of pasting drawings of door gods on their street door to ward off evil spirits, bring peace and safety and good luck. They are among the most popular guardian gods in traditional Chinese culture.

and my father made kites. In order to become a better inheritor and developer of the art of kite-making, I started at the age of 13 to study traditional Chinese arts, exemplified by traditional Chinese painting, and systematically mastered the basics of Western art. I attended the Xu Beihong High School of Art and graduated from the Xu Beihong Collage of Arts of Renmin University, with a graphic arts major.

2003 was a year of special significance.

In that year, grandfather, father and I co-founded our family brand "San Shi Zhai" kites (Three-Stone Studio). By so naming our brand, we hope that on the foundation stones of three generations of kite artists the art of kite-making passed down through the generations in our family will witness a strong, solid and steady growth. We will endeavor to make "San Shi Zhai" into a well-known and well-liked brand in and outside China. Our goal is to foster an ever wider understanding and appreciation of the art of kite-making, and the preservation and flowering of this exquisite age-old art and of the ancient culture of China.

To upgrade my kite-making skills, I studied with several master kite-makers. One of them, Mr. Tang Jinkun, an old friend of grandfather's from Tianjin, has mastered the "temple-variety or style" of the Cao Xueqin tradition of kite-making and is highly regarded in the kite community. His masterful craftsmanship in constructing kite frames is surpassed by few. In 2006, through the intermediary of my grandfather, I was able to study under Mr. Tang, who taught me everything he knew about kite-making without keeping anything back. As a result I made great strides and gained unique insights in the making of frames and special tenon/mortise constructions (FIG. 13).

In 2010, I was fortunate to be allowed to study under master kite maker Mr. Kong Lingmin, who enjoys great renown in China's kite community and whose works feature in the National Art Museum of China. Throughout these years

Mr. Kong taught me, in great detail and systematically, the esthetics of swallow kites and the art of traditional kite designs. I am greatly indebted to Master Kong for his generous guidance, which has taken me to a new level in kite craftsmanship (FIG. 14).

Driven by a consuming passion for kites, I have also called on many renowned professors in the fields of arts, design and education, heirs to intangible cultural heritage and young people with a fertile mind and exchanged ideas with them about design concepts, about life and career and I have benefited immensely from those conversations. Furthermore, I've also studied painting, calligraphy, design, photography, sculpture, ceramics, gold- and silver-smithing, lacquer, seal cutting and taichi, all of which have fed into the design and manufacture of kites and the generation of novel ideas by way of providing subject matter and inspiration.

I have always striven for the combination of traditional craftsmanship with modern science and technology and the perfect fusion

FIG. 14   *Ballet Dancer in Blue and White Pattern* by Liu Bin Hard-wing kite
In 2011, at the invitation of China's Central Ballet Troupe, the author custom designed and made this slim swallow kite "Ballet Dancer in Blue and White Pattern" based on the blue and white pattern adopted for the wardrobe of the *Nutcracker* ballet performed by the troupe. The kite is inspired by three artistic forms (blue and white porcelain pattern, the physical shape of a swallow and the pose of a ballet dancer) and the swallow tail mimics the toes of a ballet dancer. This unique kite with a ballet theme was offered later to a foreign friend as a gift.

of technique and art. While studying and mastering traditional skills, San Shi Zhai has imported CAD design concepts and equipment, such as handwritten liquid crystal display, 3-D printers, 3-D scanners and other digital tools. We have now made the transition from traditional manual design to the use of modern computer art technology to reintegrate kite structure, graphics and the manufacturing process and to fuse the designs and patterns found in a variety of Chinese arts into kite designs. This has enriched the cultural and artistic content of our kites and elevated the kite from a toy to a work of art.

With my appreciation, construction of and generally having fun with kites, and in the course of the study, innovation and development of the art of kite-making, I've found that kites have become part of my life, my daily sustenance, and have passed into my bones, into the essence of my being.

FIG. 15 *Butterfly Kite Train* by Liu Bin
Kite train
A train of soft-wing butterfly kites dancing in the blue sky

INTRODUCTION

The Chinese kite is not only an aircraft but an exquisite piece of artwork. A perfect Chinese kite must possess a finely made frame, a beautiful painted skin or sail and an ability to spread its wings and soar into the sky. The painted cover of a kite, whose theme is constituted by a combination of lines and colors, is the main aesthetic object.

Rich variety characterizes Chinese kites, and kites of different regions in China have their own distinctive artistic styles. In this book you will be able to appreciate Chinese kites with distinct southern and northern flavors.

I. Types

According to the construction of frames, Chinese kites can be divided into the following four categories.

FIG. 16 *Paradise Flycatcher* by Liu Bin
Soft-wing kite
Paradise flycatchers (*shou dai* birds) have long tail streamers and a beautiful, graceful body. Medals (*shou*), a homophone of longevity (*shou*) in Chinese, is a symbol of long life, immortality and eternal youthfulness. The *shou dai* bird kites are often painted in bright colors and come with a long tail section.

FIG. 17 *Two Immortals of Harmony and Unity* (He He Er Xian) by Guan Baoxiang
Paddle kite
This is a soft-paddle kite. *He He Er Xian* has its origin in ancient Chinese mythology. The two immortals are Hanshan and Shide, who enjoy reciting poetry to each other. The Chinese popular perception of them as a fraternal pair makes them into immortals symbolic of harmony and fraternal love, and suggestive of a life of harmony and unity.

FIG. 19 *Eight Trigrams Kite* by Liu Bin
Paddle kite
The kite takes yin-yang symbol as its theme and the colorful paper tassels help to stabilize the kite in flight.

FIG. 18 *Twin Goldfish* by Liu Bin
Paddle kite
The soft-paddle kite depicts two goldfish of different colors cuddling together. It is a kite mimicking animals in nature. Two fish placed together symbolize doubly abundant luck and good auspices.

Paddle kites: These so-called "paddle" kites are flat kites with no wings and are either soft paddles (FIGs. 17, 18) or hard paddles (FIG. 19), depending on the construction of their edges. The edges of hard-paddle kites are framed by rigid bamboo strips all around. The paddle kites can freely represent a wide range of themes and subject matter.

FIG. 20　*Owl* by Zhi Ruili
Soft-wing kite
This kite mimics an owl. Note the lifelike eyes.

FIG. 21　*Butterflies* by Liu Bin
Soft-wing kite
Butterfly kites mimic butterflies in nature; they come in bright, luminous colors and in a variety of shapes.

Soft-wing kites: These are composed of a central spine and a pair (or pairs) of wings, the upper edge of which is framed by a rigid bamboo strip and the lower edge is unframed by a bamboo strip and left flexible, hence the name "soft-wing kite". Those with one pair of wings are called "single-layer soft-wing kites" (FIG. 20), and those with more than one pair are called "multiple-layer soft-wing kites". Due to the limitations of their shapes, soft-wing kites are mostly used to represent birds and insects (FIG. 21).

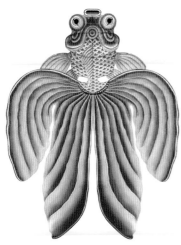

FIG. 22 *Goldfish* by Liu Bin
Hard-wing kite
This asterisk-frame hard-wing kite has its hard wings situated at the height of the gills of the fish.

FIG. 23 *God of Longevity* by Liu Bin
Hard-wing kite
God of Longevity is an immortal that symbolizes longevity in ancient Chinese mythology. The elderly man with a white beard holding a cane has an unusually long face with a prominent forehead and is ornamented with other symbols of longevity such as the peach and the gourd as well as auspicious decorative patterns.

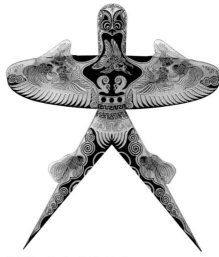

FIG. 24 *Petty Official* by Liu Bin
Hard-wing kite
Also an asterisk-frame hard-wing kite, this kite stands out with a very different pictorial theme.

FIG. 25 *Three Fish (*Xue Zu San Yu*)* by Liu Bin
Hard-wing kite
This "black pot bottom" thin swallow kite features three goldfish on each of the wings, a goldfish on the chest, and a goldfish on either side of the tail fin, thus constituting three sets of fish (*yu*), which is homophonous to surplus (*yu*, here specifically spare time). The kite exhorts people to study by making full use of spare time every day, every month and every year.

Hard-wing kites: These are generally composed of a central spine and a pair (or pairs) of wings, whose upper and lower edges are both framed by rigid bamboo strips, hence the name "hard-wing kites". Hard-wing kites are further divided into "asterisk-frame hard wings", "Chinese ideogram kites", "swallow kites" and others. Due to the endless variety of shapes, they can be used to represent different patterns and graphics.

"Asterisk-frame hard-wing kites" are generally single-layered and the bamboo

FIG. 26 *Lotus out of Water (Chu Shui Fu Rong)* by Liu Bin
Hard-wing kite
"Swallow" kites are typically Chinese hard-wing kites. This baby swallow kite is painted with graceful, refreshing lotus and butterfly patterns.

spine and other bamboo spars crossing the central spine assume the shape of the Chinese ideogram 米, similar to an asterisk (FIGs. 22–24).

The "swallow kite" is a typical Chinese hard-wing kite. Using the swallow as its theme, it has a square head with a rounded top edge; the two wings and its chest and belly are wrapped in the hard wings with a fixed shape; the swallow tail is formed by two bamboo strips in the shape of a double-tine fork. The outline of a swallow is thus complete (FIGs. 25, 26).

"Chinese ideogram kites" take the shape of a Han Chinese character, mostly in the color red. They come in symmetrical and non-symmetrical varieties. The non-symmetrical ones are harder to make because they have to be able to maintain equilibrium in flight even though they have an un-symmetrical shape (FIG. 27).

FIG. 27 *Fortune, Prosperity, Longevity and Happiness (Fu Lu Shou Xi)* by Liu Bin
Hard-wing kite
These four kites are the most typical ideogram kites; they derive their symbolism from the Chinese characters *fu* (fortune), *lu* (prosperity), *shou* (longevity) and *xi* (happiness or good auspices).

FIG. 28   *Happiness from Heaven (Xi Cong Tian Jiang)* by Liu Bin
Sifter kite
The kite uses the particular structural characteristic of a sifter kite to mimic a web woven by a spider. Spiders in ancient China had an alternate name *xi zi* (literally "bringer of happiness") due to a popular belief that when a spider drops down, it brings happiness and good luck. Therefore the kite drawn with a spider descending across its web has the name of "Happiness from Heaven".

Sifter kites: These are unique kites whose structure is comparable to that of the hard-paddle kites but their painted sails are not of one piece but are a collation of individual pieces, which are attached to the frame with glue and threads. Often they are ornamented with accessory box-like paper-pasted structures (FIGs. 28, 29).

FIG. 29   *Peacock Opening Its Tail* by Liu Bin
Sifter kite
This kite features a peacock opening its feathers, a symbol of good luck.

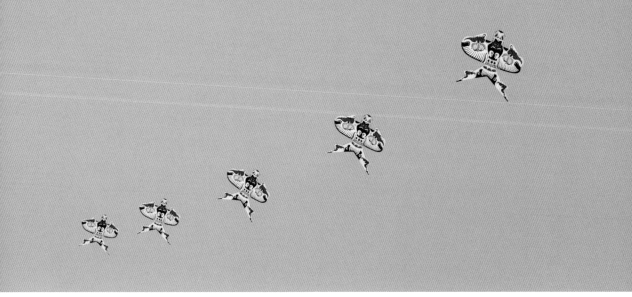

FIG. 30   *Swallow Train* by Liu Bin
Kite train
When assembling a swallow kite train, generally identical or similar swallow kites are strung together to give the train a neat, pleasing look.

FIG. 31   *Dragon Train* by Zhi Ruili (left), *Dragon Head* by Liu Bin (right)
Kite train
Dragon kite trains sway from side to side and the dragon head bobs in flight, much as a dragon in Chinese legend looks right and left as it gyrates through the air.

   Kite trains: These are made by stringing together identical or similar kite sections to form a long train. There are two common types of kite trains: "dragons" and "swallows".

   "Swallow kite trains" are relatively simple: they are formed by stringing up multiple swallow kites (FIG. 30).

   "Dragon kite trains" comprise a dragon head and a separate dragon body. The head—only one per train—is mainly decorative in nature and cannot be flown by itself. The body is composed of several independently flyable sections, which are flied as a fused single unit (FIG. 31).

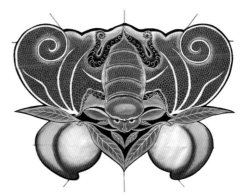

FIG. 33 *Fortune and Longevity (Fu Shou)* by Liu Bin
Paddle kite
The painted sail shows a bat (*bian fu*), homophonic to
fortune (*fu*) and a peach (symbol of longevity). A strong
aesthetic visual impact is produced both at close up and
from a distance as a result of the sharp contrast between the
red of the bat, the pink of the peaches and the green of the
leaves and the bright color tone.

FIG. 32 *Facial Pattern Kite* by Liu Bin
Paddle kite
In an example of incorporating elements of the art of Beijing
opera in kite craft, this soft-paddle kite borrows its pattern
from Beijing opera masks.

FIG. 34 *Great Mormon Butterfly* by Liu Bin
Soft-wing kite
The kite has for its theme a brightly colored Great Mormon
butterfly.

2. Aesthetics

The painted sails of kites should be a thing of beauty to be admired both at close
range and when aloft in the sky. Therefore attention must be paid in their design
to the creation of an aesthetic impact both in their static and dynamic states.
Most painted sails are on the same plane supported by the frame, therefore in
determining the composition of the graphics and patterns and the coordination of
colors, all artistic devices should be brought into play for an artistic effect unique
to kites.

Themes on painted sails: Chinese kites are rich in themes—often with
symbolic meanings—for their painted sails. Common themes include: ornamental
objects (FIG. 32), birds, good luck images (FIG. 33), insects (FIG. 34),
mythological figures (FIG. 35), fish and crabs (FIG. 36) and traditional buildings.

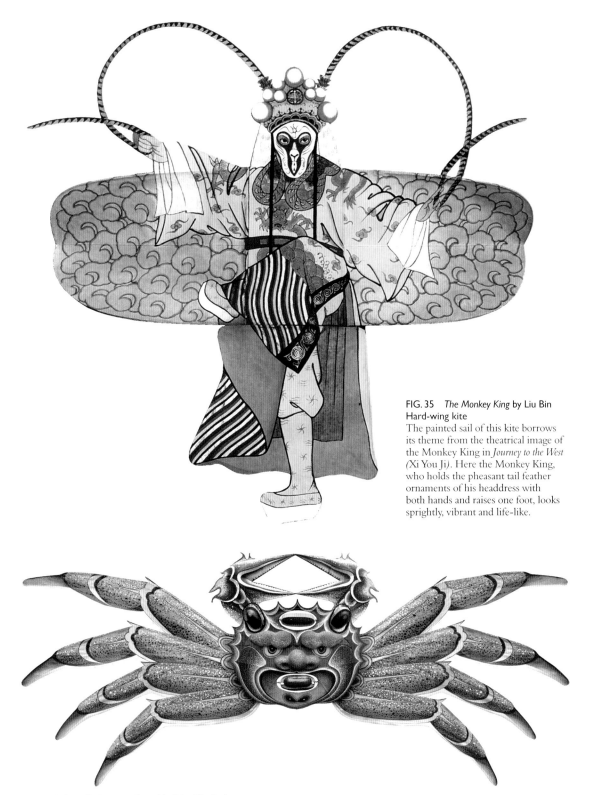

FIG. 35 *The Monkey King* by Liu Bin
Hard-wing kite
The painted sail of this kite borrows its theme from the theatrical image of the Monkey King in *Journey to the West* (Xi You Ji). Here the Monkey King, who holds the pheasant tail feather ornaments of his headdress with both hands and raises one foot, looks sprightly, vibrant and life-like.

FIG. 36 *Crab with a Ghost Mask* by Zhi Ruili
Soft-wing kite
The painted sail of this kite features a crab with a ghost's mask. A crab has eight legs, and eight (*ba* in Chinese) connotes "make a fortune" (*fa cai*). For that reason, the crab has become a symbol for wealth.

FIG. 37 *Wild Goose* by Liu Bin
Soft-wing kite
This kite mimics a wild goose and adopts the
traditional color combination of black, white and gray,
which is closer to the natural look of a wild goose.

Shapes of painted sails: When
a kite is sent aloft to high altitudes,
the details of its painted sail will
be blurred, and it's the kite's shape
and outline that can best represent
its theme. The outline and shape
of a kite should be compatible with
the image the theme is trying to
project and must serve that theme,
hence the rich variety of outlines
and shapes of the painted sails. For
example, a kite with a bird or insect
theme should have an exterior
appearance and shape consistent with
the morphology of those creatures
in nature. No matter how high or
how far away the kite is, it should
be readily recognizable as a swallow,
an goose (FIG. 37) or a goldfish kite
(FIG. 38). That's why the design of
the shape of a Chinese kite is very
important to a kite maker, which is
unique in the global kite community.

FIG. 38 *Goldfish* by Liu Bin
Soft-wing kite
Being a goldfish kite, its long tail is clearly visible high in
the sky.

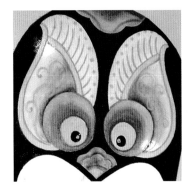

FIG. 39   The beak and eyes of a swallow account for only a small part of its body, therefore if a swallow kite is made in the image of a swallow in nature, the beak and eyes will be indistinguishable from its black head when the kite goes aloft. In this kite the eyes of the swallow are exaggerated, magnified and the black pupils are drawn off-center, giving the impression that it is looking downward, and the two sharp, up-pointing eyebrows and the pointed beak fill up the rest of the space in a natural way. The well-coordinated colors give the swallow a livelier look.

Designs and patterns on painted sails: Once the theme and the shape have been settled on, the next step is the drawing of graphics and patterns based on the shape determination. Chinese kites exhibit unique Chinese styles in the composition and color mix of their painted sails. They are often highly stylized from a realist foundation.

Sometimes decorative patterns are added, mostly drawn from the traditional Chinese culture of good auspices, to express the popular wish for good fortune. Exaggerated, highly stylized color painting techniques using bright, loud colors add to the richness of the main theme and give the kites vibrancy, earthiness and a distinctive Chinese flavor (FIG. 39). Sometimes the added decorative patterns are unrelated to the theme of the kite, but are pregnant with a meaning all its own nonetheless and will embellish or highlight the main theme. For example, "waist sections" are often added between the chest and the tail of a swallow kite. On dragon-eye goldfish kites and catfish kites, circular decorative patterns are also inserted between the gills and the head to make the transition between gills and head more natural-looking and smoother and at the same time embellish and highlight the thematic graphics (FIG. 40).

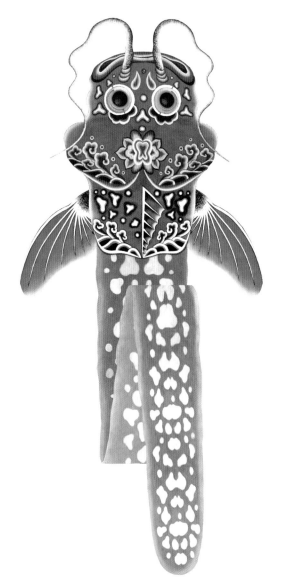

FIG. 40   *Catfish* by Zhi Ruili (painted sail) and Liu Bin (frame)
Hard-wing kite
This kite features a cute catfish with auspicious patterns at its gills.

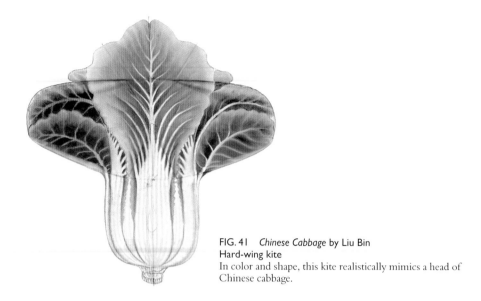

FIG. 41 *Chinese Cabbage* by Liu Bin
Hard-wing kite
In color and shape, this kite realistically mimics a head of
Chinese cabbage.

Colors of painted sails: As a rule bright and harmonious colors are used to enable kites to vividly and graphically express their chosen themes both when viewed at a distance and at close range. Basically there are four ways to manage the colors of the painted sails.

One is the realist way, which consists of painting in the natural colors of the objects mimicked (FIG. 41). For example, eagle kites are often painted in brown and black (see FIG. 2 on page 2), and dragonfly kites are colored with red, green, yellow or black (see FIG. 5 on page 4).

A second way, *xie yi* (writing of ideas, minimalist or suggestive style), employs colors unrelated to the naturally occurring objects in order to impart an intended meaning to the kite or to conjure a specific image, ambience or effect. Thus bat kites are often painted in bright red because red bat (*hong fu*) is homophonic to big fortune (*hong fu*), as in the common Chinese phrase of good wishes *hong fu qi tian*, which literally means "fortune as vast as the sky" (see FIG. 33 on page 22).

A third way uses color contrast to enhance visual effects. A swallow kite can be painted in only black and white (popularly known as the "black pot bottom"). Such a pattern with a strong color contrast is suitable for a high-flown kite. In ancient times black and white kites were flown to mourn the death of a member of the imperial clan; their use has spread because of their unique aesthetic appeal (FIG. 42). "Blue pot bottoms", kites painted in blue only, are also popular.

A fourth way enhances the visual impact by a caricatural disproportion between areas of color. Thus in a "black pot bottom" kite, the claws are made disproportionally fat so that when the kite is sent up the white claws surrounded by large areas of black will still be visible even though the white areas are much smaller than the black area of the chest (FIG. 42). The large areas of red on the "Zhong Kui (Demon Queller) Marries off His Younger Sister" kite (FIG. 43) and the large green frog clinging to the chest and belly of this "Six Unity" swallow kite (FIG. 44) vividly highlight with their large size the themes of the respective kites against the backdrop of the blue sky.

FIG. 42 *Black Pot Bottom* by Zhi Ruili
Hard-wing kite
This "black pot bottom" kite features on its chest and abdomen a dragon, which is a symbol of royalty; the bat (*fu* in Chinese) motifs on the wings and tail section represent good fortune (*fu*). By the standard of the proportion between the head width and the wing span, this is a "fat" swallow that symbolizes masculinity with the generous dimensions of its body and claws that impart a sense of virile authority.

FIG. 44 *Six Unity Swallow* by Liu Bin
Hard-wing kite
This is a "fat swallow" kite featuring a toad, ornamented with little toads at the horns and on the tail section. Sometimes water lily flowers and leaves, which are commonly seen in toads' natural habitats, are also featured. The color contrast between pink and green enlivens the drawing.

FIG. 43 *Zhong Kui (Demon Queller) Marries off His Younger Sister* by unknown artist
Hard-wing kite
The kite features Zhong Kui, his younger sister and imps that are the protagonists in a well-known folk tale, according to which Zhong Kui was a young scholar of the Tang dynasty (618–907) who scored the highest in an imperial civil service examination but was not given an official position and was instead banished to a remote corner of the realm by the emperor, whose decision was influenced by evil court ministers. Zhong Kui committed suicide out of indignation and was appointed as demon queller by the Jade Emperor, who was moved by the story of his misfortune. After his ascendance to the heavenly court of the Jade Emperor, he could not stop being concerned about his younger sister in the earthly world. One day sensing that a local bully intended to grab his beautiful sister as wife against her will, he came down to earth with an entourage of underlings and imps to carry the sedan chair, the trousseau and the lanterns, thus frightening half to death the bully setting out to pick up the unwilling bride.

FIG. 45 *Swallow with a Fish Motif* by Liu Bin
Hard-wing kite
This swallow kite with a fish motif on its chest has an
auspicious symbolic meaning of perpetual surplus because
in Chinese fish (*yu*) and surplus (*yu*) are homophonous.

FIG. 46 *Soaring Cicada and Bat (*Chan Fu Qi Tian*)* by Liu Bin
Hard-wing kite
In this thin swallow kite, a golden cicada (*chan* in Chinese)
is painted in the middle to connote "an endless succession"
(*chan lian*); a bat (*fu* in Chinese) pattern appears on each
wing tip and on the waist section to suggest good fortune
(*fu*). The two ornamental patterns together signify endless
good fortune.

FIG. 47 *Twin Swallows Side by Side* by Liu Bin
Hard-wing kite
This is a twin (side-by-side) swallow kite with two
adjoining, symmetrical heads, one male and one female.
The twin swallow kite with two swallows flying side by side
signifies conjugal harmony; the heart shape in the middle is
a symbol of husband and wife united in love.

FIG. 48 *Great Five Fortunes Swallow* by Liu Bin
Hard-wing kite
This "five fortunes" swallow is a baby swallow kite, featuring
five bats, which suggest "five fortunes", i.e. longevity, wealth,
health, virtue and a blessed end to one's life.

3. Regional Differences

Chinese kites come in a rich variety of shapes and styles, with distinct artistic flavors
depending on the regions and local customs. Here are some of the outstanding
features of the kites of four major regions in China (Beijing, Tianjin, Weifang of
Shandong province and Nantong of Jiangsu province) famous for their kites.

Kites of Beijing: Beijing kites (FIGs. 45–49) strive for unity of form and
spirit. To accomplish that, both the shape and structure of the kite and the designs
on the painted sail serve to highlight the theme of the kite. In making these kites,
attention is paid to the crafting of the frame, the application of paper or fabric
over the frame, the painting of the sail and flight worthiness. There are four
main types of Beijing kites in terms of structure and shape: paddles, soft wings
(FIG. 49), hard wings and kite trains. The designs on the painted sails must blend
well with the structure and shape. Swallow kites, of hard-wing construction,
represent the highest level of perfection and creativity among Beijing kites.

FIG. 49 *Golden Cicada* by Liu Bin
Soft-wing kite
The cicada was considered in ancient China a sacred, miraculous creature. Because it lives near the top of tall trees and survives on dew and sap only, it has become a symbol of nobility and purity. The cicada metamorphosis is considered symbolic of rebirth. The main color tone is gold, which gives the kite an elegant air.

Tip: Swallow Kites

Types: Swallow kites fall under four categories by the ratio of the length of their wing edge to the width of the head: fat swallows, thin swallows, side-by-side swallows and baby swallows. Fat swallows (FIG. 45) symbolize masculinity, with the wing-edge to head-width ratio of 7:1; thin swallows (FIG. 46) suggest femininity, with a ratio of 10:1; side-by-side swallows (FIG. 47) represent married couples, with a ratio of 16:3; baby swallows (FIG. 48) personify children, with a ratio of 5:1. Swallow kites are personified animal kites.

The frame: The head and body are usually constituted by a reverse U-shaped bamboo strip, flanked on the right and the left by a pair of hard wings and completed by a tail section formed by a reverse V-shaped bamboo strip. The ornaments on the wings and the tail section are called ornamental corner (*ba jiao*) and vary with different types and shapes of kites (FIG. 50).

Shape of the painted sail: It usually assumes the shape of a stylized swallow, with caricatures of a swallow's characteristics.

Patterns on the painted sail: A repeating pattern is often used on the waist section of a swallow kite, such as an endless repetition of the swastika 卍, of dragon pattern, of the cloud pattern, or of lotus petals. A kite can have several waist sections. These waist sections highlight the white chest and black claws of the swallow; the lines that represent the tail feathers are painted from the last of these waist sections to blend the abdominal and tail sections naturally and seamlessly. The coordination of colors gives a greater sense of compactness and beauty to the design on the painted sail (FIG. 51).

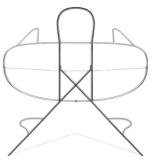

FIG. 50 Illustration of the frame of a fat swallow kite. The head and body of the frame are outlined by brown lines; the red and purple lines constitute the hard wings, and the blue lines represent the tail section; the green lines show the ornamental corners on the wings and the tail.

FIG. 51 Close-up of the waist section of a swallow kite. From bottom to top: bat pattern, 3-D zigzag line pattern, swastika pattern.

FIG. 52   *A Qilin Brings a Son* by Tang Jinkun
Hard-wing kite
According to legend, a *qilin* is a beast with a benevolent disposition, an auspicious symbol, and supposedly, like a stork, is a bringer of baby sons. People still call their smart, lovely boys "our *qilin*". Traditionally people fly this kind of kite to pray for a baby son.

FIG. 53   *Butterfly* by Tang Jinkun
Hard-wing kite
This kite has a strong Tianjin flavor with its vibrant, bright colors.

Fig. 54   *Five Fortunes Embracing Longevity* by Zhou Shutang
Soft-wing kite (a compound kite)
This kite is composed of six soft-wing kites assembled together; the constituent kites are not flyable on their own. The pattern in the middle is the Chinese character *shou* (寿, longevity), surrounded by peaches also symbolizing longevity; five bats (*fu* in Chinese) that embrace the *shou* pattern stand for good fortune (*fu*), completing the picture of five fortunes embracing longevity. The five fortunes are longevity, wealth, well-being, virtue and a blessed end to one's life.

Kites of Tianjin: Tianjin kites are characterized by their incorporation of elements of a form of colored woodblock prints in China, depicting images for decoration during the Chinese New Year (*nian hua* art), native to the town of Yangliuqing in Tianjin and Chinese traditional painting and woodblock prints, and are well-known for their bright, vibrant colors and clean, simple lines. The construction is light, delicate and nimble because no strings are used to make the frame, which is put together using only tenon and mortise connections. The designs on the painted sails feature human figures (FIG. 52), flowers and birds, insects (FIG. 53) and fish, etc. They can be asterisk-frame hard-wing kites and soft-wing kites. Ensembles made up of several soft-wing components that are not independently flyable are a specialty of Tianjin kites (FIG. 54).

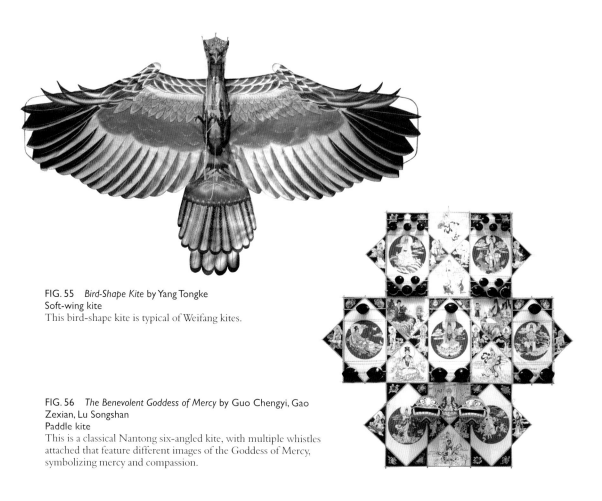

FIG. 55   *Bird-Shape Kite* by Yang Tongke
Soft-wing kite
This bird-shape kite is typical of Weifang kites.

FIG. 56   *The Benevolent Goddess of Mercy* by Guo Chengyi, Gao Zexian, Lu Songshan
Paddle kite
This is a classical Nantong six-angled kite, with multiple whistles attached that feature different images of the Goddess of Mercy, symbolizing mercy and compassion.

Kites of Weifang: Weifang kites of Shandong province are known for exquisite craftsmanship in the tying and pasting of painted sails and overall aesthetics. The styles of their painted sails bear similarities to the local woodblock prints depicting images with a Chinese New Year theme; some directly paste woodblock prints of a single color onto the frame as support before bright colors are added in. Weifang kites can be soft-wing kites or asterisk-frame hard-wing kites (FIG. 55).

Kites of Nantong: Nantong kites are known for their fine craftsmanship, visual appeal and especially their unique whistling sounds. They are predominantly *banyao* kites (*ban* means paddle and *yao* means hawk), which are hard-paddle kites, often of rectangular, square or diamond shape with six protruding angles, hence the popular name "six-angled kite" (FIG. 56). Nantong six-angled kites can be as small as one meter or less in width and length, and as large as seven meters. The kites are bedecked with rows of "whistles" of varying sizes and shapes made from bamboo, wood or nut shells; these attachments make a musical sound when the kite are sent aloft. The whistles are painted with geometric designs. There are no set conventions for the themes and content of these designs (FIG. 57).

FIG. 57   Pictures commonly seen on the whistles of Nantong kites.

FIG. 58   *Turnip* by Liu Bin, *Delta Kite* by unknown maker
Paddle kite, modern kite
A turnip kite flown in spring is a prayer for a good harvest. The triangular shape modern kite adds a modern flavor.

CHAPTER I
A HISTORICAL OVERVIEW OF KITES

Kites are constructed with a frame made of thin strips of bamboo or wood, to which light-weight silk or paper is pasted. They are easily damaged in use and do not wear well; consequently there are precious few surviving relics of kites, most of whose history can only be traced from written descriptions and drawings.

1. Early Days

The earliest kites were flying toys born of the whims of ingenious craftsmen.

We know from historical chronicles that the earliest Chinese kites were a "wooden hawk" made by Mozi (circa 468–376 BC) of the Spring and Autumn period (770–476 BC) and a "magpie" made by Gongshu Ban (also known as Lu Ban). According to the *Han Feizi*: "It took Mozi three years to construct a wooden hawk, which broke apart after being flown for one day." Mozi was in his early career a learned and skilled craftsman before he went on to become a renowned thinker and philosopher. The *Mozi*, published in the fourth century BC, contained this description: "Gongshu Ban made a wooden magpie with thin strips of bamboo and wood. It was kept aloft for three days without plunging to the ground." Gongshu Ban was a well-known craftsman in Chinese history. He was credited with the invention of various kinds of woodworking tools and venerated by generations of architects, craftsmen in the building trade and carpenters as the "founder" of their respective trades and crafts. The closeness of the dates of appearance of the chronicles of the aircraft made by Mozi and by Gongshu Ban in imitation of flying fowl, constructed with strips of bamboo and wood, and the similarity of their constructions lead us to conclude that they can be safely assumed to be the inventors of the earliest Chinese kites.

Chronicles of technical innovations in kite making were few and far between in the period of the Northern and Southern Dynasties (420–589). But it can be said for certain that as a result of the improvements in paper making technology in the Eastern Han dynasty (25–220) paper was already being used as material for the windward sail of kites. Proof of this is also found in historical records that specifically mentioned "paper hawks" or kites.

In an article about "lantern kites", Zhao Xin (birth and death years unknown) of the Tang dynasty (618–907) wrote that "I was told that Han Xin ordered the construction of kites, which he used in the battle of Gaixia as a means of

FIG. 59 *Twin Swallow* by Liu Bin
Soft-wing kite
This kite mimics two flying birds.

psychological warfare against the rival Chu troops. Another version attributed this tactic to Zhang Liang." This is the earliest record of the military use of kites in warfare. In 202 BC the Chu and Han troops fought a decisive battle at Gaixia. Han Xin ordered the construction of kites, to which were attached bamboo whistles or reeds. When these kites were sent aloft at night, they made a forlorn whistling sound in the wind, to the accompaniment of which the Han troops sang folk songs of the kingdom of Chu, causing the Chu troops to become intensely homesick and consequently to lose their will to fight.

2. Period of Growing Popularity

In the Tang dynasty, kites were mainly a form of entertainment, although the use of kites in military communications was recorded. As described in the article about "lantern kites", colorful lantern kites became popular circa 784. A lantern kite is a box kite with a cylindrical frame of bamboo strips covered by silk, gauze or colorful paper and is lit by a candle inside the box. When connected to the kite-line, the box rises into the air buoyed by the hot air produced by the burning candle and the wind lift. The flickering candlelight in the night sky had a novel visual appeal. This novel way of flying kites with interesting attachments spread and became a way for the rich and powerful to flaunt their wealth and prestige. But in dry and windy weather, these colorful lantern kites in careless hands often crashed to the ground and caused fires; this prompted the imperial court to issue a ban on these kites on safety grounds.

In the Song dynasty (960–1279) the art of painting was at a zenith. Kites that appeared in the paintings of the period offer clues to their development and the constructions and shapes and forms of the kites of those times. The painting *One Hundred Children Playing in the Spring* (Bai Zi Xi Chun Tu) by Su Hanchen depicts young children playing in spring, some of whom are shown flying a kite; the painting *Knick-Knack Peddler* (Huo Lang Tu) by Li Song (1166–1243) of the Southern Song dynasty depicts a group of children enthusiastically clustered around a knick-knack peddler and his two carriers crammed with merchandise, among which figures a paddle kite, a sure sign that kites were in wide use in Southern Song society.

Zhao Ji (1082–1135), an emperor of Northern Song dynasty, an devotee of kite flying since a child, directed the compilation of *A Collection of Kite-Making Guides* (Xuan He Feng Zheng Pu), which included descriptions of the construction of kite frames, shaping and painting, materials for kite sails (silk and paper), and multi-color graphic designs (predominantly patterns considered auspicious by the imperial court). There was no mention of hard-wing kites in the collection, a clear indication that paddle (or flat) kites and soft-wing kites mimicking flying fowl were more in vogue in those times (FIG. 59). The Collection helped popularized kite flying and making.

We find 12th century chronicles mentioning kite-flying contests: in his *Wulin Reminiscences* (Wu Lin Jiu Shi, a wide-ranging collection of reminiscences about folks, events and customs of Lin'an, also known as Wulin, the capital of the Southern Song dynasty), the Southern Song man of letters Zhou Mi wrote: "Youths flew kites on a bridge, vying to cut someone else's kite-line with their own. Whoever ended up with a severed kite-line was declared a loser."

In an old ruin dating to the Jin dynasty (1115–1234), a bronze mirror depicting kite-flying has been unearthed. The back of the mirror is decorated with four picture groups, each of which shows two persons flying a kite (FIG. 60). Of the many bronze mirrors unearthed, this is the only one that bears the kite motif and is the earliest object with a representation of kites of antiquity found so far in China.

In the Yuan dynasty (1279–1368), kite flying was a popular pastime. The poet Xie Zongke from Jinling (birth and death years unknown) described kite flying in one of his poems: "Children flying kites trample the wild grass underfoot as they chase each other around in play. Even though they retrieve their kites after each flight, eventually the kite-lines break and the kites fly away. The children watch with envy the clouds in the sky, wishing their breakaway kites would stay aloft like the clouds."

FIG. 60   This bronze mirror unearthed in Huaide, Jilin province has on its back images of kite-flying.

FIG. 61 An illustration by Sun Wen for *A Dream of Red Mansions*, in a collection hosted at Lüshun Museum in Liaoning province. The kites seen in the drawing are all soft-wing kites.

3. Golden Age

Xu Wei (1521–1593), man of letters of the Ming dynasty (1368–1644), described in a poem a box kite in the form of a bird with a frame built by lashing bamboo strips together and covered with hemp cloth.

In the Qing dynasty, the famed writer Cao Xueqin (circa 1715–1763 or 1764) published *Nan Yao Bei Yuan Kao Gong Zhi*, an important work of reference on kite flying as a hobby and pastime in Beijing in the mid-Qing period. It includes mnemonic verses giving instructions on the tying, pasting and painting of kites and a catalogue of kites in color. Cao Xueqin, author of *A Dream of Red Mansions* (Hong Lou Meng), referred to kites at several points in the novel, such as in Chapter 70, which listed eight kinds of kites: the "Butterfly", the "Beauty", the "Phoenix", the "Big Fish", the "Crab", the "Bat", a train of "Seven Swallows", and a kite in the shape of the Chinese character of "happiness" (*xi*, 喜). It can be inferred from these descriptions that the soft-wing kite was already popular in that period and was developing into a category of its own (FIG. 61). The mention of the train of "Seven Swallows" kites suggests that the appearance of the category of trains, or kites strung up together to form a single kite, could not be later than 1760. The reference to another new type of kites—the swallow kites—in a different edition of *A Dream of Red Mansions* is an indication that hard-wing kites predate 1792.

In 1793, drama/opera playwright Li Dou (?–1817), coeval of Cao Xueqin, wrote in *Yang Zhou Hua Fang Lu*, a chronicle of the social, economic and cultural life of the town of Yangzhou in that period: "Kite flying has reached its heyday in the Ming and Qing dynasties. Many of the kites produce a sound through the vibration of strings. Kites maintain their balance with an appropriately attached tail section. The largest kites can reach one *zhang* (unit of length equivalent to about 10 feet) in width and the length of the tail section can be as long as three *zhang*. The most commonly seen kites are rectangular in shape; the rest are in the shapes of the crab, the centipede, the butterfly, the dragonfly and the Chinese characters 福 (pronounced *fu*, meaning fortune) and 寿 (pronounced *shou*, meaning longevity). The kites are often exquisitely made by craftsmen. Some flown at night have a lantern tied to the tail section. Some are composed of three or five kites strung together." This description suggests that up to the early Qing period, the main category of kites was still the paddle type and in addition to the *banyao* kites or whistling kites, kites mimicking real life creatures were already very common.

The Jiu Pu written by Mr. Jin Junshao in 1897 is the earliest technical treatise on kites in China. It gives detailed descriptions of the techniques of tying, pasting, painting and flying kites and divides kites into the six categories of paddle kites, soft-wing kites, hard-wing kites, side-by-side swallows, centipedes and accessaries. Jiu Pu also mentions foldable kites in China, which represented an important breakthrough in kite craft that facilitated storage and portability as well as fostered the spread of the all kinds of kites and the techniques of their manufacture.

The Qing dynasty also witnessed the publication of detailed accounts of trade in kites. Di Jing Sui Shi Ji Sheng, published in 1758, is a chronicle of the customs and ways of life of the people of Beijing, the imperial capital. A description of a kite market appears in the book: "The paper kites of the imperial capital are exquisitely made. Some sold at the Liulichang market cost several ounces of gold each." In the Daoguang era (1821–1850) of the Qing dynasty, Fang Shuo gave the following account: "During the Spring Festival in Beijing, most streets are deserted and quiet. Only in a locality about two *li* (unit of length equivalent to about 500 meters) from Liulichang do we see a steady stream of carriages and horses all day long … there one finds all kinds of wares, such as clay figurines, bonsais, kites and ornamental lanterns. The market is abuzz with shoppers." This account of the bustling market outside Liulichang corroborates the importance of kites in commerce in that period.

In the Qing times, Liulichang became a mecca for shoppers and tourists every year from the 1st to the 15th of the 1st lunar month. Kite-making gradually developed into a trade. The wide open spaces around Liulichang at the time made it a natural choice for people flying kites. A poet described in one of his poems the popular tradition of buying and flying kites at Liulichang around the time of the 15th of the 1st lunar month.

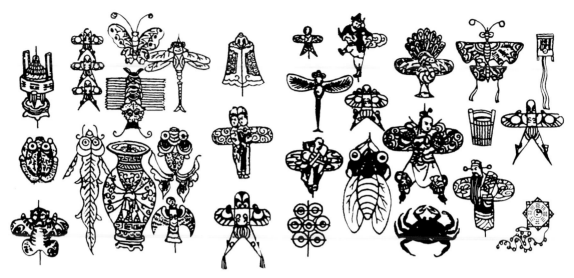

FIG. 62   One of the surviving pages of *Collection of Kites of Beiping* published in the republican era. Beiping is today's Beijng.

4. Modern Times

Kites, written by Chen Zefeng and published in 1934 by Zhengzhong Publishing House of Nanjing, explained for the first time the structural characteristics of China's traditional hard-wing kites. In Chapter 4 "Categories of Kites and Techniques of Kite-Making" he supplied the structural details of different kinds of kites, such as the "eagle", the "butterfly", the "goldfish" and hard-wing Chinese ideogram kites (FIG. 62).

Advances in photography made it possible to keep pictorial records and data of kites. Photos have survived from the republican period showing stalls selling kites; it can be inferred from the pictorial information that the swallow kites and hard-wing kites were the main category of kites flown in Beijing in that period (FIG. 63).

In the republican period, the different schools of kites with which we are familiar today were in their formative periods in four main localities that produced kites: Beijing (FIGs. 64–66), Tianjin, Weifang of Shandong province and Nantong of Jiangsu province.

Beijing has two traditions of kite-making of note, represented respectively by Ha Guoliang and Kong Xiangze. The Ha-style kites made famous by Ha Guoliang, the founder, are well known in Beijing. He laid down the specifications, templates and dimensions and proportions of his kites that became the standards for four generations of followers after him. At the 1915 Panama Pacific International Exposition held in San Francisco of the United States, Ha Changying, the keeper of the Ha tradition of kite-making, won a silver medal and letter of recognition for the "butterfly",

FIG. 63   A stall selling kites in the republican era

FIG. 64 *Colorful Butterflies Attracted to the Flowers (Cai Die Xun Fang)* by Liu Bin
Hard-wing kite
This is a hard-wing swallow kite. Based on the criterion of the ratio between the width of the wing span and the width of the head, this is categorized as a "thin" swallow kite that symbolizes femininity. Butterflies, gourds and gourd vines bedeck the head, wings, the ornamental corners and the tail section; they symbolize "abundant progeny". Butterfly (*die*), homophonous to small melon (*die*), which with its long vines suggests an unbroken line of a multitude of descendants. The chrysanthemum and butterfly patterns on the chest of the swallow hint at "the butterflies' love for the flowers".

FIG. 65 *Little Tiger* by Liu Bin
Hard-wing kite
This kite depicts a little lovely tiger squatting.

FIG. 66 *Little Nezha Fights Great Dragon King (Ne Zha Nao Hai)* by Liu Bin
Hard-wing kite
This is a typical Beijing kite. It uses a Chinese folk tale as the theme.

"dragonfly" and "crane" kites he brought to the exposition. The Ha-style kites are known for their well-made frame, standard dimensions, simple, traditional styling and meticulous, elaborate painting.

Kong Xiangze was the restorer of the Cao Xueqin tradition of kite-making. When he studied under his Japanese sculpture teacher Kagami, he borrowed from Kaneda, a friend of Kagami's, a handwritten manuscript of *Fei Yi Zhai Collection* (Fei Yi Zhai Ji Gao), from which he was able to copy by hand a section on kite-making (Nan Yao Bei Yuan Kao Gong Zhi) . He also learned kite-making techniques from master kite craftsmen of the time Zhao Yushan, Guan Guangzhi and Jin Zhongnian. Later, in collaboration with Jin Fuzhong, a kite maker of the Qing court, Kong Xiangze restored the Cao Xueqin tradition of kite-making and named kites made in that tradition "Cao-style kites". Cao-style kites emphasize the synergy of painted sail designs and kite shapes, vivid likeness to objects mimicked and the dynamic beauty of kites in flight.

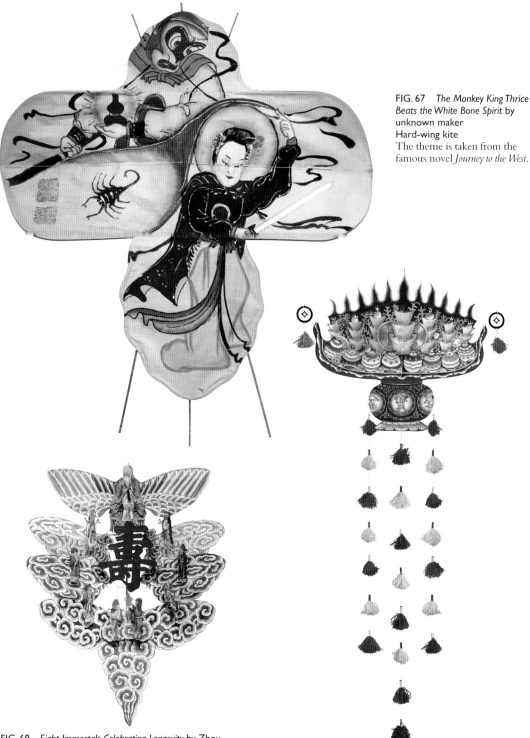

FIG. 67   *The Monkey King Thrice Beats the White Bone Spirit* by unknown maker
Hard-wing kite
The theme is taken from the famous novel *Journey to the West*.

FIG. 68   *Eight Immortals Celebrating Longevity* by Zhou Shutang
Soft-wing kite (a compound kite)
This kite is formed with nine soft-wing kites. The central Chinese character *shou* (longevity) is surrounded by seven immortals standing on seven auspicious clouds, with an eighth immortal sitting on a celestial crane, completing the picture of "eight immortals celebrating longevity".

FIG. 69   *Treasure Bowl* by Iang Jinkun
Hard-wing kite
The main theme of the painted sail is a treasure bowl filled with money and treasures. According to legend, the treasure bowl is an overflowing source of treasures and therefore is a symbol of accumulating wealth.

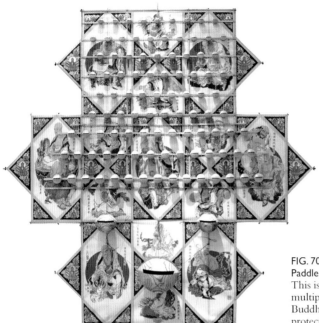

FIG. 70 *Eighteen Arhats* by Guo Chengyi
Paddle kite
This is a classical six-angled whistling kite ornamented with multiple whistles painted with the eighteen arhats, who, in Buddhist belief, are stationed permanently on this earth to protect the Buddhist faith.

Weifang of Shandong province is historically famous for fine handicrafts. Kite makers of Weifang incorporate elements of Chinese traditional painting and woodblock pictures celebrating the lunar New Year in their kites, creating a unique style. No systematic information about Weifang kites prior to the 1980s has survived. From 1984 on, an annual International Kite Festival has been hosted in the city of Weifang, which was voted the Kite Capital of the World in 1988. Weifang has thus been put on the world map and its kites have achieved enormous fame. Weifang is best known for its dragon-head centipede kites and human figure kites (FIG. 67).

Tianjin also boasts a very distinctive school of kite craft, embodied by Wei Yuantai, nicknamed "Wei of the kites". Wei Yuantai was born in the Tongzhi era (1862–1874) of the Qing dynasty. He opened a workshop specializing in kite making (named Wei's Changqing Zhai Kite Shop). At the 1915 Panama Pacific International Exposition, he won a gold medal for eleven fine kites handmade by him. Tianjin kites stand out for their vivid likeness, elegant colors and fine craftsmanship (FIGs. 68, 69).

Nantong of Jiangsu province is best known for its whistling kites. Nantong kites date back a long time. Cao Xueqin, author of both *A Dream of Red Mansions* and of *Fei Yi Zhai Collection* on kites, grew up in Jiangsu and devoted a section of the latter work to a comprehensive description of Nantong kites. Before 1978, Nantong kites were still a burgeoning folk handicraft with no comprehensive system or records. It was only later that craftsmen and scholars embarked on a systematic chronicle of kite-making in Nantong and published a series of books on kites. Nantong kites have become known outside China as a distinctive form of handicraft with a style all its own (FIG. 70). Nantong whistling kites are characterized by harmonious colors, pleasing sounds and balance in flight.

FIG. 71 A distinct feature of Chinese kites is the use of bamboo for their frames. Bamboo is not only light in weight but also strong. This is the back side of the *Paradise Flycatcher*, see FIG. 16 on page 15

CHAPTER 2
TOOLS AND MATERIALS FOR KITE MAKING

There is an old proverb which says that "good tools are half the work"; good tools and materials are essential in the making of fine kites. This chapter gives detailed descriptions of the frame, the painted sails, the tying and pasting and the flying of kites.

Whether a kite can be launched or flown successfully depends to a large degree on the frame, which is traditionally assembled with bamboo strips. Bamboo is superbly suited to the making of kite frames because it is light, strong, flexible and tough, and can, upon being heated, be bent into desired shapes that will not change after the heat is removed. The painted sail bespeaks the artistic merit of the kite; it has a lot in common with Chinese traditional painting, and employs basically the same set of tools and techniques. Pasting and tying represent the steps of integrating the frame, the painted sail and the kite-line reel and require special tools and materials. Toward the end of the chapter we will describe the tools needed for flying kites.

1. The Frame

With the selection of the right bamboo and its proper storage and by working on the bamboo with suitable tools and harnessing the special characteristics of bamboo, a kite maker can create a fine frame for the kite.

Materials for the Frame

If you look at the cross section of a bamboo stem, you'll see that it consists of the skin, and the pulp that has a green outer layer possessing good flexibility and a yellow inner layer that is hard and brittle, which is normally removed for making kite frames (FIG. 72).

Choice bamboo comes with good flexibility and toughness. In China, kite makers usually choose moso bamboo (*mao zhu*) and Neosinocalamus affinis (*ci zhu*) that mainly grow in the provinces of Fujian, Jiangsu, Zhejiang and Sichuan. For ease of storage, freshly harvested bamboo stems about 8 meters long are cut into 1.5-meter sections, which are then split into 5 mm wide planks or 3 mm wide strips, with the yellow inner layer of the pulp retained. The planks and strips are then left to dry in a dry location shaded from the sun and resistant to moisture. These bamboo materials are ready for use when

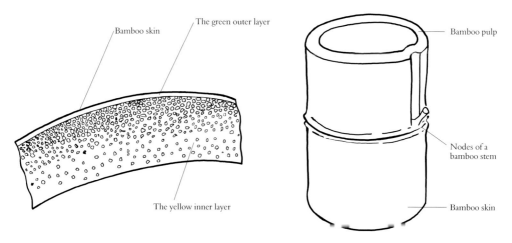

FIG. 72   Bamboo stem

they naturally dry and turn yellow in two or three years (FIG. 73). The freshly cut bamboo stems contain a large amount of water and therefore have a green color and poor flexibility; they cannot be easily made to keep their shape when they are bent into the desired forms in the heating process. If frames are assembled with strips made from these fresh bamboo sections, the frames are apt to bend out of shape when the kite is launched because of the uneven moisture vaporization in different parts of the bamboo subjected to varied wind forces. Nor should the bamboo be too dry, for that would mean insufficient flexibility and toughness and when subject to stress and heating during the heating process, the strips are liable to break. Normally bamboo that is too young and tender or too old and tough is unsuitable for the making of kite frames.

When choosing bamboo for a kite frame, account has to be taken of the size of the kite (FIG. 74). A most important consideration is the thickness of the bamboo and the length of the internodes. Bamboo materials that are thick (5–10 mm) and have short (20–40 cm) internodes are suited for making bigger kites (transverse span ranging from 1 to 1.3 meters); bamboo with shorter internodes requires more processing. Bamboo materials that are thinner (2–3 mm) and have longer (50–80 cm) internodes are unsuited for making large kites. Bamboo with longer internodes does not require

FIG. 73   Bamboo planks and strips

FIG. 74 *Butterfly* by Liu Bin
A distinct feature of Chinese kites is the use of bamboo for their frames.
Bamboo can be clearly seen on this kite.

special processing and therefore entails less work. Kites that are less than one meter across can sometimes have frames made with bamboo sections that do not contain any nodes.

Before being used to make a frame, the bamboo strips must be closely screened. Lengthwise scratches on the skin of the bamboo section can be avoided when splitting the section into strips. But if the wounds are crosswise on the skin of the bamboo section, it should be thrown out because the crosswise wounds weaken the bamboo and when the bamboo is split into very thin strips during processing, they tend to break when the frame is assembled.

Cutting Tools

Bamboo hatchet: To section bamboo into larger planks.

    Single-bevel knife: For shaving bamboo.

    Double-bevel knife: For splitting and scraping bamboo.

    Knife for electricians: For splitting bamboo.

    Mallet: To aid in splitting thicker bamboo. With the knife making a starting cut in the bamboo section, hitting the back of the knife with a mallet will help.

    Side-cutting pliers: For snipping thin bamboo strips. Choose flush cutting pliers, otherwise the bamboo strips will have a jagged edge after being nipped.

    Wood saw: For cutting wood or bamboo. Get a large saw for cutting larger, thicker pieces of bamboo and a smaller one for cutting thin strips.

    Wood file: For coarse cutting of bamboo materials. It is a flat file with a triangular pyramid-shaped front end featuring rough teeth.

FIG. 75 *Lord Rabbit* by Liu Bin
Paddle kite
This kite uses a Lord Rabbit, a symbol of Mid-Autumn Festival, as its theme.

    Steel file: For smooth cutting of bamboo materials. It is in the form of a stick with a rectangular pyramid-shaped front end featuring dense, fine grooves.

    Cutting Mat: A cutting board placed on the workbench to protect the knife and the table surface. It is hard enough to ensure a clean cut but not so that it would hurt the blade. When cutting bamboo materials on the board, the knife will not slip and the surface is not reflective of light. The cutting mat is strongly tolerant of knife cuts; with proper use, it will not be visibly scored in the first year of use or two. Make sure it does not come in contact with oil or grease, which might cause physical damage to it.

Heating Tools

Needle-nose pliers: For clamping the bamboo material when it is being bent to desired shapes over heat.

    Candle: Used for shaping bamboo strips. Due to its smaller, cooler flame, it is suitable for heating medium-thickness or thinner strips. It is safe and easy to use.

    Alcohol burner: Used for shaping bamboo strips. Due to its stronger, hotter flame, it is used more for heating thicker strips. Care should be taken for safe use; avoid overturning or breaking the burner, which may cause a fire.

Cutting Tools

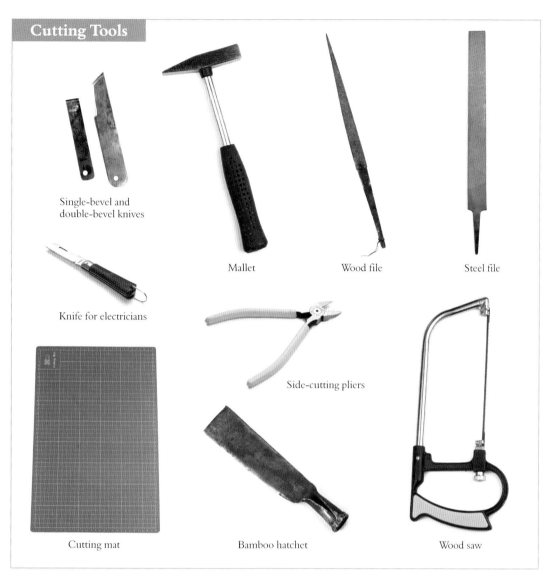

Single-bevel and
double-bevel knives

Mallet

Wood file

Steel file

Knife for electricians

Side-cutting pliers

Cutting mat

Bamboo hatchet

Wood saw

Heating Tools

Needle-nose pliers

Candle

Alcohol burner

Auxiliary Tools

Straight edge: Kites are aircraft and require precise measurements in their manufacture; straight edges are used to measure lengths.

Tape measure: With its greater length, it can be used to measure longer objects.

Sharp-nose tweezers: They can be used instead of the hands to hold materials when making frames for mini kites.

Pencil: For drawing plans and drafts and making marks on the bamboo strips.

Craft knife: It is used for cutting paper or in making mini kites.

Scissors: They are used for cutting painted sails and cutting cords and strings.

Canvas cloth: It is placed over the kite maker's legs when shaving bamboo strips.

Grindstone: Used for sharpening knives.

FIG. 76   This is the wing part of the "Colorful Butterflies Attracted to the Flowers" swallow kite (see FIG. 64 on page 39), showing the precise measurements in the manufacture of the straight and curved edges.

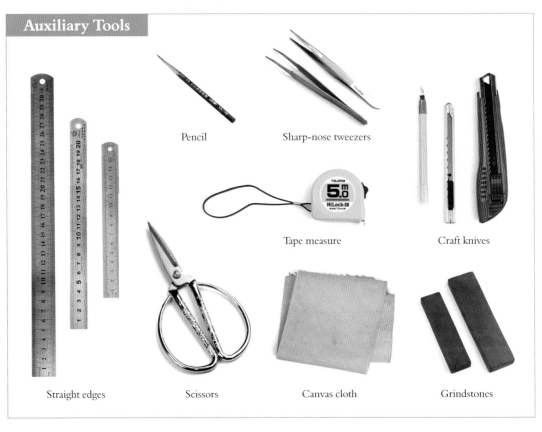

Auxiliary Tools

Pencil

Sharp-nose tweezers

Tape measure

Craft knives

Straight edges

Scissors

Canvas cloth

Grindstones

Fig. 77 *Peacock Opening Its Tail (*Ping Kai Que Xuan) by Liu Bin
Hard-wing kite
This fat swallow kite features in the middle of its painted
sail a peacock opening its feathers and butterfly and peony
patterns on the wings and the tail, expressing the wish of
parents for their daughter to find a desirable husband.

FIG. 78 *Double Fish* by Liu Bin
Paddle kite
The double fish represent good wishes for vitality and
growth in one's family. It is a common motif of Chinese
kite design.

FIG. 79 *Monk Pig* by Liu Bin
Paddle kite
The painted sail of this kite borrows its theme from the
theatrical image of the Monk Pig in *Journey to the West*. His
two ears which are exaggerated, add to the richness of the
main theme.

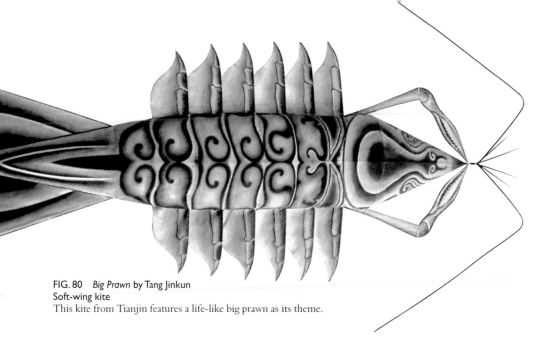

FIG. 80 *Big Prawn* by Tang Jinkun
Soft-wing kite
This kite from Tianjin features a life-like big prawn as its theme.

2. Painted Sails

Chinese kites are distinguished by uniquely Chinese graphics and patterns on their painted sails.

Materials for Painted Sails

Painted sails are mainly made of paper and silk. The criteria for selection are:

1) Quality of the material: Kites with silk for their painted sails are usually fine art crafts or high-end merchandise;

2) Characteristics of the material: Kites with sails made of silk, which is stronger than paper, can stand stronger winds for a longer duration;

3) Ease of painting and coloring: Silk sails need to be ironed constantly throughout the painting process; this entails more work, whilst paper sails can be ironed after the painting is done or do not need ironing at all, thus incurring savings in time and effort;

4) Materials' intrinsic advantages in highlighting the themes of the kites and enhancing aesthetic, visual impact: For instance, silk, which allows more light to pass through than paper, can be used for the painted sail of dragonfly kites to mimic the diaphanous nature of the dragonfly wings.

Materials for painted sails need to be soft, tough, and have good absorbent qualities and resist wear and tear. With technological advances, new types of materials of excellent serviceability as painted sails and at reasonable prices have been coming on the market and kites made with these materials can often keep for dozens of years or longer.

Xuan paper: Mainly used for the painted sails of hard-wing mini kites 40 cm in size or smaller. There are many varieties of xuan paper but only a few of them are suitable for kites. Look for those that are soft, tough and tear resistant. There are two types of xuan paper: the raw xuan paper (*sheng xuan*) and ripe xuan paper (*shu xuan*). The ripe xuan paper is ooze-resistant and can be painted by adding washes of ink and color layer by layer, and is therefore suited for the meticulous painting style. Painting on raw xuan paper, with its strong water absorbency, and the tendency for the ink on it to blur and ooze out, is a challenge and requires experience in the use of this kind of paper and in controlling the water content of the painting brush.

Materials for Painted Sails

Silk

Nonwoven fabric

Dupont Tyvek

Xuan paper

Crepe paper

Silk: Main material used by China's imperial court for making kites in the past, and in high-end kites today. Finer details and more vibrant colors can be achieved on silk than possible on paper. Silk is also longer lasting; silk kites made for the Qing imperial court have survived to this day and are on view at the Palace Museum in Beijing. Make sure to select silk that has potassium alum worked into it during production because, firstly, alum-treated silk has qualities similar to ripe xuan paper that suit it to being painted on and there is less likelihood for the colors to run and ooze out on it; secondly, untreated silk lack stiffness and is more permeable to wind, and it is more difficult to launch kites made with untreated silk or to keep them in flight. Silk easily creases during the painting process and requires constant ironing to maintain evenness of the surface.

Nonwoven fabric: A modern material that comes in different thicknesses, suitable for painted sails of kites one meter or less in size. Its advantages are softness, strong resilience, good absorbency, tear resistance and reasonably low prices. There will be some oozing of the colors but the problem is more manageable than in raw xuan paper.

DuPont Tyvek: A modern material, suited for large hard-wing kites over one meter in size. Its advantages are low wind permeability, sturdiness, wear-resistance and durability. Due to the smoothness of its surface, acrylic paints have to be used; colors applied on it will retain their vibrancy and freshness for long periods. Its surface remains even during the painting process but the inability to fold and crease it to make markings and to use an iron on it is a disadvantage.

Crepe paper: A textured paper of various colors, used in ornaments and attachments that help the kites keep their balance in flight.

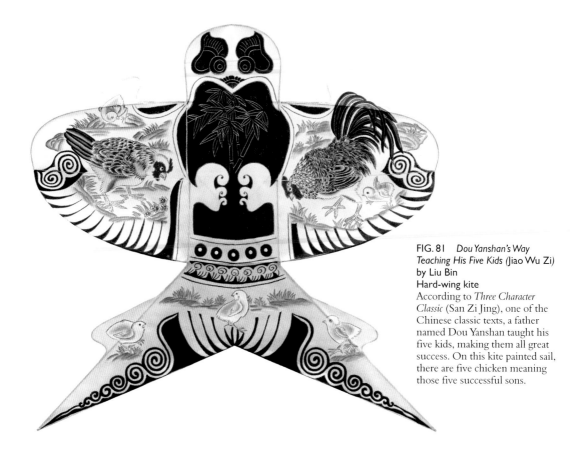

FIG. 81 *Dou Yanshan's Way Teaching His Five Kids (Jiao Wu Zi)* by Liu Bin
Hard-wing kite
According to *Three Character Classic* (San Zi Jing), one of the Chinese classic texts, a father named Dou Yanshan taught his five kids, making them all great success. On this kite painted sail, there are five chicken meaning those five successful sons.

Painting Tools

Calligraphy brushes: There are two main types of brushes—soft and hard. Hard-hair brushes have harder tips and are suitable for drawing lines; soft-hair brushes have softer tips and are used for applying colors. It's a good idea to have brushes of varying sizes at hand for painting kites of different sizes.

Paint brushes: For painting the kite sails; you'll need one small and one large brush.

Felt mat: A thick mat made from wool, normally white in color, with an even surface resistant to water penetration. It is used as support for paper or fabric sails to be painted and prevents water soluble paints on the sails from staining the table surface and in turn smudging the painted sails.

Palette: Normally made of plastic or porcelain. It is compartmentalized into several receptacles for mixing multiple colors.

Brush washer: A large vessel used for rinsing calligraphy brushes; the height of its side should be greater than the length of the heads of the brushes. Fill the bowl with clean water and rinse off the brush before switching colors.

Brush stand (or rest): A rack with multiple notches in which to rest calligraphy brushes not in use, to prevent the pigments on the brushes from rubbing off where they are not supposed to.

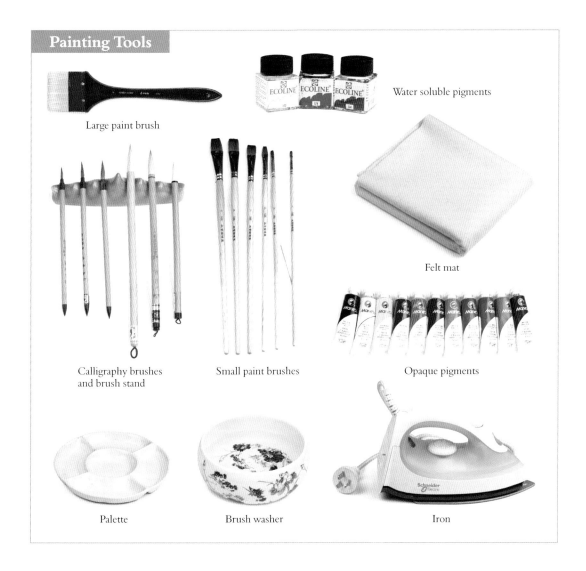

Painting Tools

Large paint brush

Water soluble pigments

Calligraphy brushes and brush stand

Small paint brushes

Felt mat

Opaque pigments

Palette

Brush washer

Iron

Paper weight: To keep in place paper that is being written or painted on; usually made of metal or stone, it also helps maintain the smoothness of the paper being painted on. You could use grindstones as paper weight.

Pigments: Two types of pigments are used for painting kites—water soluble pigments that produce bright colors and have a better translucent quality that makes the painted sails look light and diaphanous; and pigments that are opaque (such as gouache and acrylics), and when several coats of these are applied, the colors will have a thick and dense quality but the kite thus painted will have an increased weight. In practice the two types of pigments are used in combination depending on the requirements of the design of the kite to take advantage of their different characteristics. It is worth pointing out that when painting on silk sails, both types of pigments are often used in the same kite to achieve contrast by taking advantage of the translucent and opaque qualities of the two types of paints, thus creating a vivid, eye-catching visual impact.

Iron: To smooth the sail of the kite.

Tools for Tying and Pasting

Needle

Shuttle   Cotton thread   Emulsion glue   Superglue

3. Tying and Pasting

Shuttle: Capable of spooling a large amount of string when putting together a kite frame.

Cotton thread: To connect the frame to the kite line reel. Never use a plastic or nylon fishing line to attach to a kite for it is liable to come loose and separate from the kite.

Needle: Usually needed in the tying of the bridle lines of a kite.

Emulsion glue: Binds tightly but dries slowly, normally taking upwards of 5 hours to set; used mainly for gluing bamboo strip to bamboo strip and for gluing bamboo strips to kite painted sails.

Superglue Superglue: A fast drying adhesive that sets in seconds. It is used mainly to bind bamboo strips to strings. When applied to a knot, it can quickly solidify the binding string on the bamboo strips. When used in combination with an emulsion glue, the result is even better.

FIG. 82 *Ten Thousand Generations of Progeny (Zi Sun Wan Dai)* by Zhou Shutang Soft-wing kite (a compound kite)

This kite from Tianjin is a large compound kite featuring a gourd in the center. The gourd (*hulu* in Chinese) is a recurrent symbol in Chinese folk art because it sounds like *fu lu*, meaning "fortune and prosperity" and the branches and leaves of the gourd plant are called *man dai*, which is homophonous to *wan dai*, meaning literally "ten thousand generations" and the many seeds in a gourd complete the metaphor of "ten thousand generations of progeny". The five butterflies surrounding the gourd are decorative.

FIG. 83 *Three Abundances and Nine Granted Wishes (*San Duo Jiu Ru*)* by Liu Bin
Hard-wing kite
Apart from the bat pattern meaning happiness and fortune, this kite is also painted with nine *ruyi* (granted wishes) scepters, representing good wishes.

4. Kite Flying

Kites are aircraft; kites of different sizes and shapes can fly in the sky only when they are equipped with the proper kite lines and reels.

Kite Lines

The selection of suitable kite lines is important. Generally speaking, they should fulfill the following requirements:

Great tensile strength: A kite often is subject to stress many times its weight when in the air, with winds blowing at the kite and air resistance to the lines all ultimately pulling at the kite lines. For that reason kite lines must be strong enough to stand such pulls.

Light weight: For kite lines with equal tensile strength, choose those with the least weight per unit of length. This varies greatly with the materials of the lines. This is however not the only criterion; toughness and wear resistance must also be taken into account.

Toughness and wear resistance: Due to its frequent winding and unwinding and friction against obstructive objects, the kite line must be tough and wear resistant.

Low aerodynamic drag: Generally speaking, smoother, slicker lines have less

Plastic kite string holder

Double-braid nylon lines

Kevlar lines

Fishing lines

Pentagonal and hexagonal spool-type reels

Spoke-type reel

String winder

Spoke-type reel with a spindle handle

Plastic reel

Metal clasp

Steel-rimmed reel

aerodynamic drag.

Low elasticity: Including tensile and torsional elasticity; high tensile elasticity in a kite line affect the ability of the kite flyer to control the flight of the kite in a timely manner, due to the delay in the transmission of the flyer's action to the kite caused by the elasticity of the line. High torsional elasticity is even more disadvantageous for kite flyers: when the cumulative torsion in the line exceeds the elastic limit, the sudden burst of the cumulative force will be relayed to the kite and cause it to spin out of control and plunge to the ground. The use of no-twist swivels can minimize such undesirable incidents.

There are three commonly available kite line materials that may be chosen according to the size of the kite.

Double-braid nylon lines: Low price, high tensile strength but poor wear resistance, suitable for small and medium-size kites.

Kevlar lines: A fire-resistant material with high tensile strength, wear and heat resistance.

Fishing lines: High strength, low aerodynamic drag, but poor wear resistance. Due to its extraordinarily small cross-sectional size, a fishing line has a greater risk of causing hand injuries. When flying larger kites connected to a fishing-line, protective gloves must be worn to avoid the line's pressing on the hands, causing obstruction to blood circulation or hand injuries. Due to the high elasticity of the fishing-lines, they tend to stretch to a greater extent when temperatures rise and tend to become brittle and break easily at low temperatures.

Kite Line Reels

The requirements for kite-line reels are ease of paying out and winding in the kite line, light weight and portability, solid construction and durability. With technological advances, more products are coming on the market that fulfill these requirements outstandingly.

Hexagonal or pentagonal spool-type reels that turn on a handle: Chinese kite flyers traditionally use these devices.

Spoke-type reel: Most kites can be flown from this kind of winder that is fast with letting out and reeling in the kite line.

Steel rimmed reel: Suited for flying larger kites, able to stand greater force than most.

Plastic reel: Suited for commonly flown kites.

Spoke-type reel with a spindle handle: Suited for flying mini kites.

Plastic kite string holder: Suited for flying simple, mini kites.

String winder: For super-size kites.

Metal clasp: For connecting kite string to the kite; they facilitate assembly and disassembly.

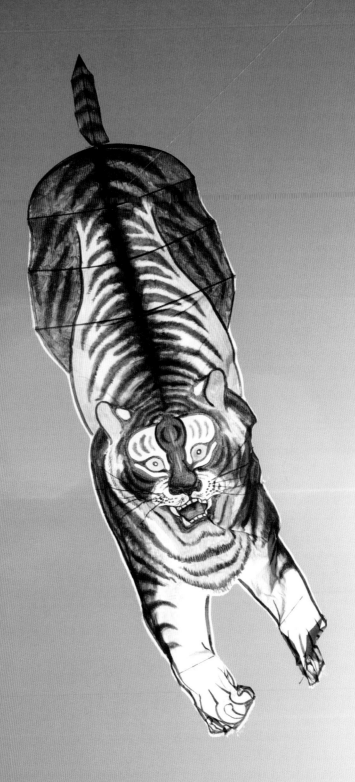

FIG. 84 *Tiger* by Liu Bin
Paddle kite
This flying tiger seems to come alive and appears to be pouncing on you.

CHAPTER 3
BASICS OF KITE CONSTRUCTION

T he construction of a Chinese kite goes through the four stages of frame assembly, painting, pasting and tying.

The first step is the building of the frame, which consists of processing of the bamboo materials, heating and shaping of the frame components, binding and assembling these bamboo strips to form the frame.

The second step consists of painting the skin or sail of the kite; the theme of the kite is painted on the sail for the kite to produce an artistic, aesthetic visual effect in flight (FIG. 85).

The third step consists of pasting the painted sail onto the frame.

The fourth step consists of tying the kite through a string to the kite line reel.

After learning the basics, a kite maker should also learn to read the kite plans to become familiar with the details of the frame construction.

1. Assembling the Frame

There are three steps to the assembly of the frame: firstly, the preparation of the materials, i.e. preliminary treatment of the bamboo materials; secondly, the making of components, i.e. further processing of the bamboo components into construction members that meet the requirements of the kite frame being made; thirdly, the assembly of the components by gluing and binding the various bamboo strips to form the desired frame.

FIG. 85 *Butterfly with Clouds and Bats* by Liu Bin
Hard-wing kite
This kite shaped like a butterfly ornamented with auspicious clouds and bats to convey good wishes for good fortune, happiness and harmony.

Preparation of the Materials

Before the final assembly of the frame, the following process of cutting and heating has to be completed. The bamboo material has to be sawed to the desired lengths and shaved to the specified thickness; if there are nodes they need to be trimmed or filed smooth; lastly the exterior skin of the bamboo needs to be removed for a smooth surface.

Single-bevel and double-bevel knives are used during the entire process; they are used for splitting, shaving and scraping. After preliminary preparation of the bamboo materials, the bamboo strips need to be trimmed and smoothed, made flat and straight and cut to the specified lengths. If a bamboo strip has quirks or uneven spots on it, they can be corrected by heating. Visually inspect every bamboo strip to see if it is of even width and thickness; if not, trim it with a knife to achieve even width and thickness. If the length of the strip is not right, cut off excess with a pair of side-cutting pliers. Make sure the bamboo strips come out of this preparatory process in neat shape, and of even width and specified length.

FIG. 86 *Ten Thousand Generations of Fortune and Prosperity* by Liu Bin
Hard-wing kite
This kite features big and small gourds, meaning "fortune and prosperity". The branches and leaves of the gourd plant means many generations. With these five chubby babies, this kite implies "ten thousand generations of fortune and prosperity".

• Cutting Bamboo to Desired Length: Sawing and Nipping

There are two ways to cut bamboo to desired lengths. Sawing: Wood saws are used on larger bamboo components and only during the stage of bamboo preparation. Nipping: Side-cutting pliers are used, normally for cutting bamboo strips less than 1 cm in thickness.

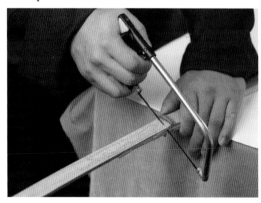

Sawing

Nipping

• Processing Bamboo to Specified Thickness: Splittig

"Splitting" means dividing lengthwise a large section of bamboo or bamboo strip. The bamboo material close to the skin is tougher and therefore the knife starts the cut closer to the pulp. If the bamboo component is already of the right thickness, the inside skin of the bamboo pulp still needs to be scraped off. There are different ways of splitting to achieve specific results: basic split, wiggle split, fingernail split and pierce split.

Basic split: Cut the bamboo lengthwise; strike the blade on the back gently with a mallet if needed. The bamboo will split along the grain of the bamboo fibers, and the splitting line will go off center if the fibers are not straight. It is therefore necessary to correct the crookedness beforehand by heating the bamboo, then split the bamboo to the end.

Wiggle split: In the process of splitting bamboo, the splitting line sometimes goes off center. This can be corrected by twisting the knife and wiggling the bamboo half away from the veer. In this way the split can be guided. This technique can also be used to make bamboo strips of uneven width.

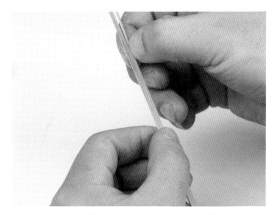

Fingernail split: This technique is used to split bamboo strips less than 1 mm thick that have straight fibers; it is particularly suited for making mini kites. First make a crack with the blade along the bamboo strip, then split it with a fingernail along the crack. When working with very thin bamboo materials, this technique is faster and more precise than splitting solely with a knife.

Pierce split: Pierce the bamboo strip in the middle with a knife, and make an opening by wiggling the blade; it is used to change the shape of a bamboo strip, often used when making strips for the "insertion" method of assembling bamboo strips for the frame (see page 68).

• **Processing Bamboo to Specified Thickness: Shaving**

"Shaving" means cutting with a blade at an angle, mainly to remove excess or unwanted parts from a bamboo strip. It gives more precision than "splitting". There are four ways of shaving: draw-shaving, shaving away from oneself, shaving while pulling the bamboo strip and hand-held shaving.

Draw-shaving: Facing the work table, the kite maker places the bamboo strip lengthwise on the cutting mat, holds the near end of the strip with one hand and shaves the strip horizontally toward oneself with the single-bevel blade held in the other hand at a predetermined angle to the strip.

Shaving away from oneself: Done in a similar manner of draw-shaving, the only difference being the direction the knife moves during the shaving process, in this case the knife moves away from the kite maker.

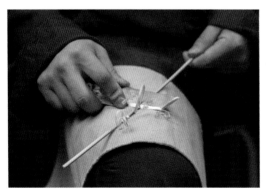

Shaving while pulling the bamboo strip: Commonly used in trimming long bamboo strips. The seated kite maker places the bamboo strip on a thick canvas cloth draped over his thigh, holding the near end of the strip with one hand and keeping the single-bevel knife stationary against the strip with the other hand while pulling the strip to accomplish the shaving action. Make sure the knife is kept at a constant, predetermined angle to the strip.

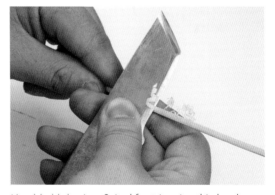

Hand-held shaving: Suited for trimming thin bamboo strips. The knife-holding hand moves the blade against the strip with its fingers wrapped around the back of the bamboo strip to better monitor the thickness of the strip as it is being shaved to make sure the desired thickness is achieved. This is precision work.

FIG. 87 *Fortune Comes Before Our Eyes (Fu Zai Yan Qian)* by Liu Bin
Paddle kite
This kite is drawn with two bats and three ancient Chinese coins. The
Chinese name of the bat is *bian fu* and *fu* shares the pronunciation of
"fortune" in Chinese; the coin with an eye in the middle, *yan qian* in
Chinese, is a homophone of "before one's eyes" and the two motifs
combined connote "fortune comes before your eyes".

• Processing Bamboo to Specified Thickness: Scraping

"Scraping" requires greater precision than "shaving". In this method, the
trimming is done with the blade held at right angles to the bamboo. It is used
often in the final stage when the finishing touches are applied, including the
removal of the green skin to reveal the yellow pulp of the bamboo, giving the
frame a neat, pleasing appearance. There are three ways to scrape bamboo
strips: level scraping, pull scraping and hand-held scraping.

Level scraping: Sit facing the work table, place the
bamboo strip lengthwise on the cutting mat in front
of you; with one hand holding the strip down, take
a double-bevel knife in the other hand and keep the
blade at right angles against the strip and begin scraping
away from you.

Pull scraping: Used more often for trimming longer
bamboo strips. In a seated position, place the bamboo
strip on a canvas cloth draped over your thigh, holding
the near end of the strip, take a double-bevel knife
in the other hand with the blade kept at right angles
against the strip and repeatedly pull the strip while
keeping the blade stationary.

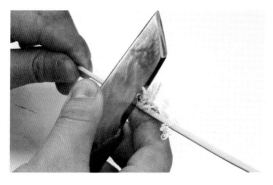

Hand-held scraping: Better suited for trimming very thin
bamboo strips. The knife-holding hand moves the blade
against the strip with its fingers wrapped around the back
of the bamboo strip to better monitor the thickness of
the strip as it is being scraped to make sure the desired
thickness is achieved. This is precision work.

• Heating

Heating bamboo over an alcohol burner, a candle or some other heat source is a technique used to shape bamboo strips into various desired forms. Keep the bamboo strip at an appropriate distance to the flame depending on the intensity of the flame to avoid kindling or burning the bamboo being heated. Heating is usually done for one of two purposes: bending and tempering.

Heat bending is heating a bamboo strip over a flame to soften it for later bending and shaping; heat bending can be done for any of the four sides of the strip. It is done normally with the bamboo strip held in one hand or, to prevent burns to the hand, with the aid of a pair of needle-nose pliers. Heat tempering can increase the strength of the bamboo strip and help it to retain its shape.

Heat bending: Heat the backside of the bamboo strip over the flame at the point to be bent; make sure to heat it evenly and not to concentrate the heat on any particular spot. After the bamboo is softened by heat, bend it with both hands downward; after the flame is removed and the strip cools down, it will stay in shape. Repeat if necessary until the desired result is achieved. Never overheat, otherwise the bamboo may get burnt or catch fire.

Heat tempering: To temper bamboo by heating, heat frame components that require added strength evenly; if the components also need to be shaped by heating, do it at the same time as the tempering procedure. Only when the oils and moisture in the bamboo are removed by heating will the bamboo strip and the frame stay in shape.

• Trimming and Filing

Trimming and filing the bamboo nodes is performed to straighten and smooth the bamboo strip at the nodes to give it a neat, pleasing appearance, as well as to fulfill the requirements of the shape and construction of the frame. After bending the bamboo strip by heating, file it at the nodes to create a smooth, even surface.

Trimming the nodes: Heat and bend the bamboo strip at the nodes on both sides to straighten the fibers at the joints.

Filing the nodes: First use a wood file to smooth down the protuberances on the skin of the bamboo and then a steel file to trim the bamboo; turn the strip over and similarly smooth down the protuberances on the reverse side. After the nodes are filed down on both sides, the strip should become straight and even.

FIG. 88 *Journey to the West* by Liu Bin
Hard-wing kite
These kites are the four characters in *Journey to the West*, one of the Four
Great Classical Novels of Chinese literature. They are Master Tripitaka,
Monkey King, Monk Pig and Friar Sand.

Making the Components of the Frame

During the materials preparation process, the shapes of the bamboo components are roughly fixed. Next comes the finishing of components that have special requirements. Here we will explain three special procedures used at this stage: the symmetrical splitting of a bamboo strip, the making of a central spar and the making of a one-piece wing edge.

• Symmetrical Splitting

The symmetrical splitting of a bamboo strip is employed when making two symmetrical components of the frame and is aimed at maximizing the identicalness of the two components. It combines the use of splitting, scraping and shaving techniques and is the most basic technique used in constructing a frame.

1 Make a bamboo strip whose width is more than twice the width of the needed components. Heat and bend the strip into the desired shape.

2 With a single-bevel knife, split the bamboo strip along the center line into two equal parts.

3 First trim one of the two equal parts to the specified width by employing shaving and scraping techniques.

4 Place the other strip against the one that has been treated in step 3 as a template and trim it to the exact same shape and size using shaving technique.

5 Trim it to the exact same shape and size by employing scraping technique.

6 When both strips have been thus trimmed, they should conform to the same specs.

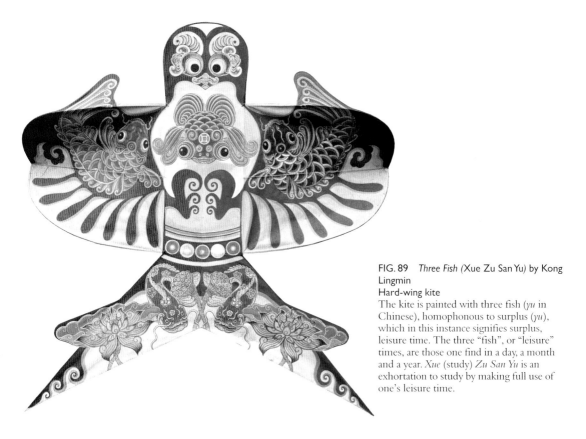

FIG. 89   *Three Fish (*Xue Zu San Yu) by Kong Lingmin
Hard-wing kite
The kite is painted with three fish (*yu* in Chinese), homophonous to surplus (*yu*), which in this instance signifies surplus, leisure time. The three "fish", or "leisure" times, are those one find in a day, a month and a year. *Xue* (study) *Zu San Yu* is an exhortation to study by making full use of one's leisure time.

• Making a Central Spar

In the making a central spar, the upper part is kept more rigid than the lower end of the spar. It is done before the heating process.

Employing the techniques of shaving and scraping, trim the central spar in such a way that it tapers from top to bottom so that it is more rigid at the upper end and becomes more flexible toward the lower end.

• Making a One-Piece Wing Edge

In the making of a one-piece wing edge, the flexibility at the two ends of the wing spar must be symmetrical. It is done before the heating process.

Employing the techniques of shaving and scraping, trim the one-piece wing spar so that the widths at the two ends are identical, thus ensuring symmetrical flexibility at the wing tips.

Assembling the Components

When all the bamboo strips are ready, they will now be assembled into the desired frame by using glue and string. Here we will explain the techniques of "attachment" and "lashing", which are independent of each other and yet closely related, because the frame components made with these techniques come together in the completed frame.

There are six ways of attachment: overlap, insertion, slit-end, double slit-end, kneeling and splicing. Splicing is connecting two bamboo strips of equal width and thickness.

There are two basic types of lashings used to bind the bamboo strips: diagonal lashings and shear lashings. For higher efficiency, a shuttle can be used.

Tip: Using a Shuttle

A shuttle for knitting fishing nets can be used to facilitate threading the string in and out of the spaces between the bamboo strips when lashing the bamboo strips together for the kite frame. Tie the string around the notch at the bottom of the shuttle and its bamboo tongue and use the shuttle as the working end of the string, passing it back and forth between the spaces.

• Types of Attachment: Overlap, Insertion, Slip-End, Double Slit-End and Kneeling

Overlap: Two bamboo strips are overlapped at right angles.

Insertion: A bamboo strip is inserted into a slit cut in the middle of another strip.

Slit-end: Cut a slit into the end of a bamboo strip and insert another strip crosswise into the slit end.

Double slit-end: Connecting two bamboo strips with split ends inserted into each other.

Kneeling: Heat and bend one end of a bamboo strip into a desired curve and lash it at the curved end to another bamboo strip.

• Types of Attachment: Splicing

1 With a pencil, mark the points at which the two bamboo strips are to be attached.

2 Shave the ends into identical bevels.

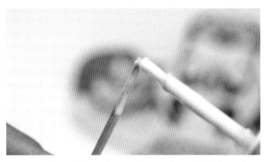

3 Apply emulsion glue on the surface of the bevels.

4 Splice the two strips at the beveled surfaces.

5 Temporarily lash and fix the spliced strips together until the glue sets.

6 After the glue sets securely, shave off the temporary lashing with a knife by using draw-shaving. Trim the connection to make it neat and smooth.

7 Wrap several turns of string around the connection in shear lashing manner. Done.

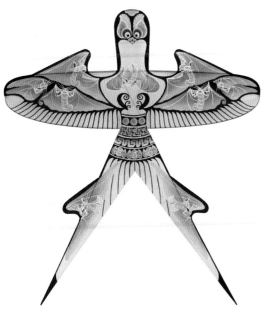

FIG. 90   *Three Abundances and Nine Granted Wishes (San Duo Jiu Ru) by Liu Bin*
Hard-wing kite
This kite takes green as its theme color.

FIG. 91   *Three Abundances and Nine Granted Wishes (San Duo Jiu Ru) by Liu Bin*
Hard-wing kite
This kite takes pink as its theme color.

• Types of Lashing: Diagonal Lashing

Diagonal lashings are used to bind two strips crossing each other at right angles; they are commonly used when two strips are attached overlapping each other, when one strip is inserted through an opening in another, and when one strip is inserted in the end slit of another.

1 Wrap a turn around the starting end of the string to secure it down.

2 Wrap an equal number of turns around both diagonal crossings.

3 Finish with an overhand knot.

4 Apply a small amount of superglue on the lashing to secure it. Done.

• Types of Lashing: Shear Lashing

Shear lashings are used to bind two strips placed end to end with string neatly and densely wrapped multiple turns around the strips; they are most suited for attaching one strip with a bent knee-like end to another strip (kneeling type attachment) and for two strips spliced together.

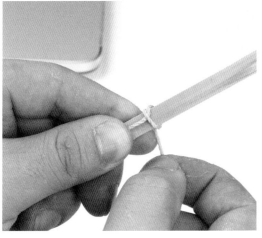

1 Wrap a turn around the starting end of the string to secure it down.

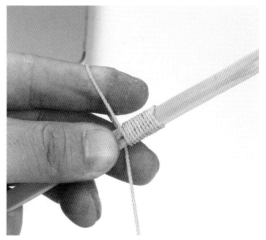

2 Wrap a sufficient number of turns around the work.

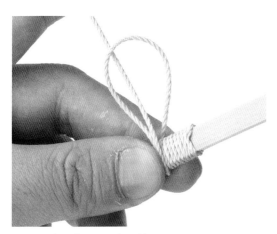

3 Finish with an overhand knot.

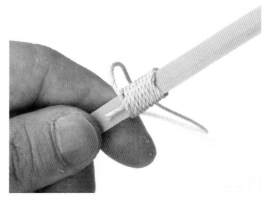

4 Done. Apply superglue on the lashing to soak it; when the glue sets, the lashing will be secure.

Tip: Air Dry the Frame

Bamboo materials may still contain moisture even several years after being harvested. To avoid problems, air dry the assembled frame for several days or even months before painting and pasting the sail on the frame.

2. Painting the Sails

Kite sails can be painted with easy-to-use oil pastel sticks or watercolor brushes; alternatively the *gong bi*, or the minute and laborious technique of traditional Chinese painting, can be employed. Here we will only touch on the aspects of the complex *gong bi* technique that relate to the painting of kite sails.

The painting of kite sails involves the making of a line drawing and the application of pigments.

• Making a Line Drawing

A line drawing outlines in black ink the patterns to be painted.

A hard-hair brush for line drawing with a fine tip is often used to make line drawings.

Most kites have left-right symmetry in the patterns drawn on their sails. To ensure such symmetry, draw half of the pattern on paper, wait for the ink to dry before placing another sheet of paper over it and trace the pattern to produce the other half.

• Application of Pigment

The application of pigments comes after the line drawing is done and there are two techniques for doing that: flat wash and graded wash. Flat wash leaves an even color. Graded wash enables the gradual transitioning of one color to another or a gradual fading.

After the colors are applied, it is often necessary to go back and sharpen the outlines with appropriate pigments (often but not limited to black, white and gold), to render the picture more distinct and the composition clearer, and to a small extent, cover up coloring slipups. When applying graded wash between different colors, you need to use several brushes each loaded with a different pigment to transition to a neighboring color.

Flat wash: Painting over a specific area with one pigment, leaving an even color, without any trace of painting strokes.

Graded wash: You need two brushes, one loaded with pigment and one soaked with clear water. Paint with the pigment brush. Before the pigment dried go over the pigment with the clear water brush repeatedly to spread and even out the color. You can use a paper napkin to soak off excess water and adjust the amount of pigment on the brush. With appropriate control of the water in the brush, a good effect can be achieved.

Tip: How to Hold a Brush

There are different postures for holding the brush depending on the size of the painted areas.

Basic posture: Hold the brush vertical over the paper with your index and middle fingers and the thumb in such a way that the brush moves freely in all directions; control the movement of the brush with the fourth finger and the little finger. Keep the fingers close together to ensure a firm grip and keep the palm open and relaxed to ensure freedom of movement of the brush.

Wrist rest posture: Hold the brush as in the basic posture, with the wrist and the elbow resting on the table for support. In this posture the movement of the brush is somewhat constrained but it makes precision painting easier.

Raised wrist posture: With the wrist suspended in the air and the elbow resting on the table as support, the brush can move more freely than in the wrist rest posture but it is harder to control the movement of the brush.

Raised elbow posture: With both the wrist and the elbow suspended in the air, the brush enjoys the greatest degree of freedom of movement in this posture, but also faces the greatest challenge in exercising control over brush movement, which can be achieved only with diligent practice.

3. Pasting the Painted Sail on the Frame

After completing the construction of the frame and the painting of the sail, the next step is pasting. When pasting a kite, first cut the painted sail to the shape of the frame, leaving a margin extending out around the frame. The width of the margin depends on the size of the kite. For a kite one meter across, leave a margin about one centimeter wide.

Pasting is done in two steps: pasting on the frame and pasting around the edge.

• Pasting on the Frame

In the first step the back of the painted sail is glued to the outer edge of the frame.

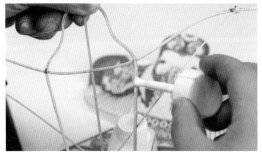 

1 Apply emulsion glue evenly on the upside of the frame. Avoid using too little or too much glue; too much glue retards drying. Place the frame on the painted sail, making sure it is correctly positioned.

2 Press down on the frame to aid adhesion, all the while kneading and stretching in all directions until the sail is smooth and snug against the frame.

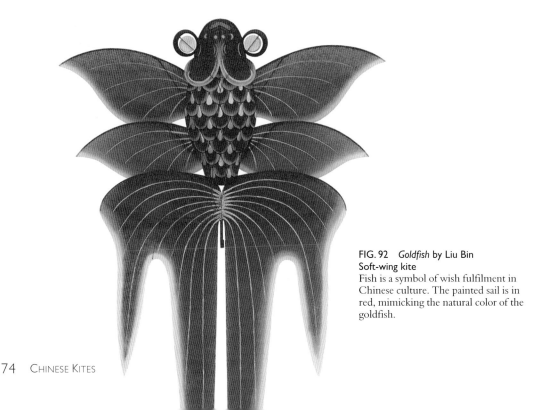

FIG. 92 *Goldfish* by Liu Bin
Soft-wing kite
Fish is a symbol of wish fulfilment in Chinese culture. The painted sail is in red, mimicking the natural color of the goldfish.

• Pasting around the Edge

In the step of pasting around the edge, you can either paste the margin of the sail around the edge or trim away the margin of the sail extending beyond the frame to leave the fine bamboo work exposed.

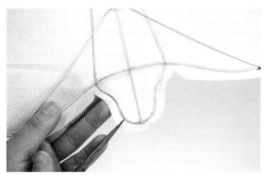

Pasting step 1: Where the outer edge of the frame is curved, make notches in the corresponding part of the sail margin stretching beyond the frame.

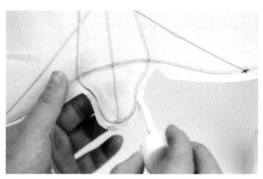

Pasting step 2: Apply glue to the margin of the painted sail extending beyond the frame.

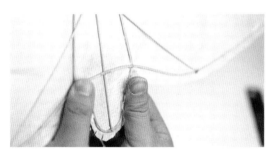

Pasting step 3: Glue the margin to the frame.

Pasting step 4: The result is as shown. For sections of the outer edge of the frame that are straight lines, there is no need to notch the corresponding part of the margin of the painted sail when pasting it down around the edge.

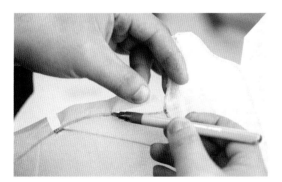

Trimming step 1: After the glue dries, use a craft knife to trim away the margin extending beyond the frame.

Trimming step 2: The result is as shown.

4. Tying

In this step the kite is tied to the reel with a kite line. This is the first preparatory step before the launching of the kite in the air. When connecting the kite to the reel, make sure the strings are securely tied and in such a way as to maintain the balance of the kite when in flight.

• Knots

Four knots are used in this step.

Overhand knot: Basic knot involving a single string.

Eye knot: Take a bight in a rope, hold the two strands together and tie them in a simple overhand knot, allowing a portion of the bight to extend like a loop.

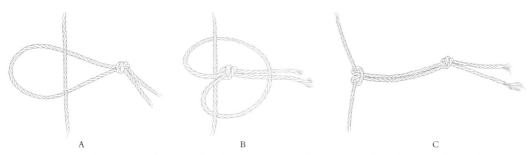

A   B   C

Lark's head knot: Where a second string is placed across the loop of an eye knot, then the knotted end of the eye knot is brought over the second string and threaded through (under) the loop. Pull tight to complete the lark's head knot. Follow the order of A, B, C above to complete the knot.

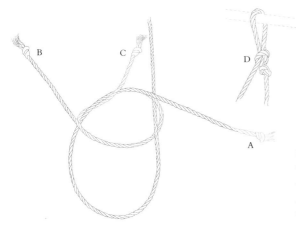

B   C   D

A

Double overhand knot: Starting from an overhand loop, draw the end upward through the loop to form the first overhand knot, bring the end across the loop, and bring the end up through the loop again to form the second overhand knot, following the order of A, B, C as shown in the figure. Draw tight to complete the knot as shown in D.

• Connecting the Kite to the Reel

Depending on the type of kite, there are three ways to connect the kite to the reel.

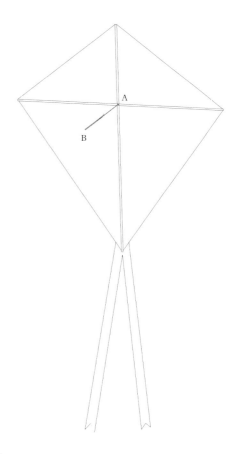

Single-string connection: Attach a single string to the frame with a double overhand knot at point A of the frame and make an eye knot at point B to be connected to the end of the kite line from the reel.

Two-string connection: Two strings are used in this connection; one string is attached to the central spar at points A and B (exact positions of the points vary with individual kites) with a double overhand knot at either point. Make an eye knot with the other string at point D; trim off loose ends and tie a lark's head knot with the loop of the eye knot to point C of the string connecting A and B. The loop is for connection to the end of the flying line from the reel.

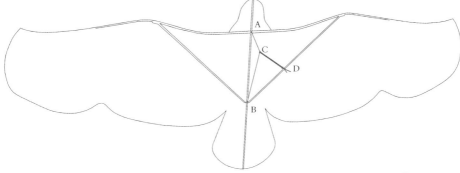

Three-string connection: Connect one string to the upper part of the kite at points A and B with a double overhand knot at either point; the exact positions of A and B depend on the individual kites. The second string is connected to point E in the lower part of the kite and to point C at the exact center of the first string; the exact position of E is kite-specific, a double overhand knot is used at E and a lark's head knot is used at C, thereby creating a tight knot at D, with CD forming a loop. Make an eye knot at point G of the third string, cut off excess line and make a lark's head knot with the loop at point F of string DE. The loop is for connection to the end of the flying line from the reel.

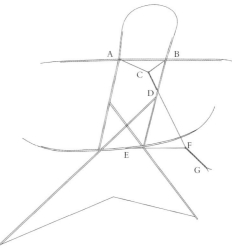

FIG. 93   *Seagull, Black Pot Bottom* and *Fairy* by Liu Bin
Different kinds of kites fly in the sky.

5. Learn to Read a Kite Plan

It is important to know how to read the structural plan of a kite frame. A frame has a front and a back; the kite plan shows the side visible from below when the kite is in flight, i.e. the side with the bridle lines attached to it. We will illustrate with the plan of an eagle kite.

The proportional relationship between the overall length, width and thickness of the kite frame is fixed and therefore to change the size of the kite, you need only proportionally change the values of the dimensions. Now that you know how to read kite plans, the step-by-step illustrations in the following Chapter 4 will help you to create kites with a distinct Chinese style and flavor.

• Plan of an Eagle Kite

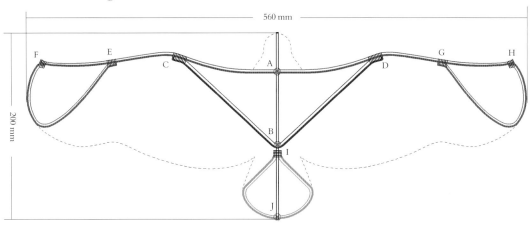

The different colored lines show the configuration of the components of the frame and their shapes. The lengths and widths of the components are given. The letters of the alphabet show the points where the components meet.

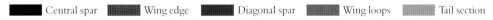

■ Central spar   ▦ Wing edge   ▦ Diagonal spar   ▦ Wing loops   ▦ Tail section

Three different kinds of line symbols represent different meanings.

═══ One thin line above a thick line: The thick line represents the skin side of the bamboo, the thin line represents the pulp side; together they represent a cross sectional side view of the bamboo material.

═══ Two thin lines: This symbol represents the pulp of the bamboo and means the bamboo material has its inside facing up.

‥‥‥‥ A dotted line represents the edge of the painted sail of the kite.

How the components are tied is also shown.

‖‖‖‖‖‖ A band of densely spaced vertical lines indicates a shear lashing.

⊗   A cross inside a circle indicates a diagonal lashing.

Indication of where the bridle lines are attached to the frame.

●   A red dot indicates a point where the bridle lines are attached to the frame.

FIG. 94 *Catfish* by Liu Bin
Hard-wing kite
This kite features a red catfish as its theme. The catfish has whiskers,
a big mouth and a big head, features that are clearly discernible from
below even when the kite is high up in the sky. The eyes, gills and the
mouth of the catfish on this kite are surrounded by small fish, which
symbolize "perennial abundance".

CHAPTER 4
EXAMPLES ILLUSTRATING THE MAKING OF CHINESE KITES

I n this chapter we describe the steps in making eight Chinese kites: four
paddle kites, including three soft ones (a phoenix kite, a goldfish kite
and a Monkey King facial pattern kite) and one hard-paddle kite (an Eight
Trigrams kite); two soft-wing kites, including one single-layer kite (an
eagle kite) and a multiple-layer kite (a butterfly kite); two hard-wing kites,
including one asterisk-frame hard-wing kite (a petty official kite) and one
swallow kite (a good fortune and longevity swallow kite).

Of the eight kites, the paddle kites are the easiest to make; next come,
in order of the ease of making them, the soft-wing kites, followed by the
hard-wing kites. We will start with the easier ones.

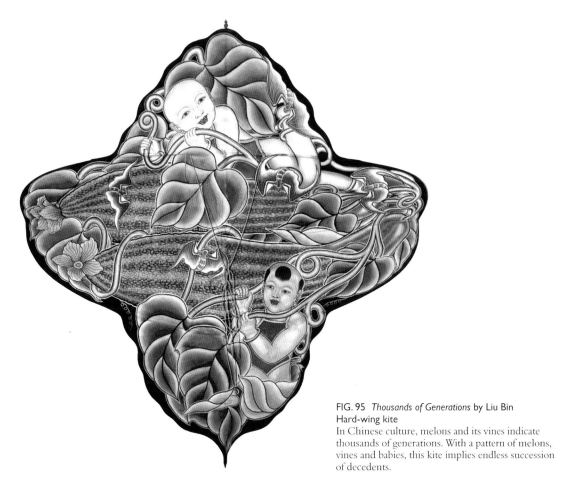

FIG. 95 *Thousands of Generations* by Liu Bin
Hard-wing kite
In Chinese culture, melons and its vines indicate
thousands of generations. With a pattern of melons,
vines and babies, this kite implies endless succession
of decedents.

1. Phoenix Kite

The phoenix is a fabled bird and a kind of totem in Chinese culture. The mythological phoenix rises from the ashes and is credited with an ability to be cyclically regenerated or reborn; it has always been an auspicious symbol.

This kite is a typical soft-paddle kite; its painted paper sail is not secured onto a rigid frame but rather has its four sides left flexible. The frame is a simple cross; two tail streamers cut from the same material as the sail, glued to the backside of the painted sail, serve not only to help maintain the kite's equilibrium in the air but also add grace to its flight.

Construction of the Frame

The construction of this kite is quite simple. It consists of a central spar and a wing edge crossing each other. One feature of this frame is the absence of lashing at the point of intersection of the two pieces. Due to the kite's light weight and reduced drag, gluing the two pieces together suffices to ensure the sturdiness of the frame.

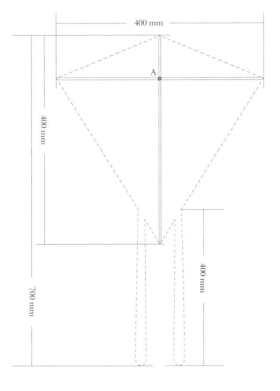

■ Central spar: length 400 mm; upper width 2 mm, thickness 1.5 mm; lower width 1.5 mm, thickness 0.7 mm

▦ Wing edge: length 400 mm; width 1.8 mm; thickness 3 mm

═ The inner surface of the bamboo facing up

--- Border of the painted sail

● Point where a bridle line is attached to the frame

Making the Frame Components and Their Assembly

Take two bamboo strips of equal length; make the wing edge with one, using the technique of "making a one-piece wing edge" explained before; make the central spar with the other strip, using the technique of "making a central spar" explained before. Assemble the two bamboo strips into a cross shape, using the "overlap" technique of attachment explained before and glue them together. The frame is completed.

Painting the Sail

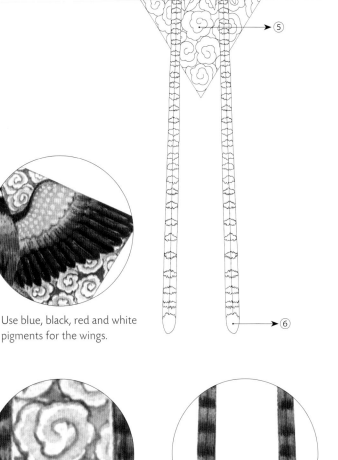

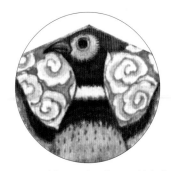

1 Use blue, red, yellow and black pigments to paint the head of the phoenix.

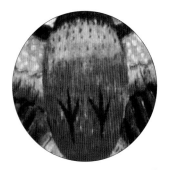

2 Use red and black pigments for the body of the phoenix.

3 Use blue, black, red and white pigments for the wings.

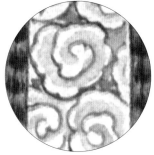

4 Use green, red and black pigments to paint the tail.

5 Use blue and white pigments to paint the background to evoke a picture of white clouds floating in an azure sky.

6 On a separate sheet of white paper, paint the two tail streamers with red and brown pigments.

Pasting

1 Apply glue on the frame.

2 Spread the painted sail over the frame, smoothing the sail with your hands, and cut off excess paper.

3 Cut off excess unpainted paper around the tail streamer.

4 Follow the kite plan to glue the tail streamers to the underside of the kite.

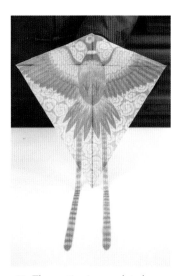

5 The pasting is completed.

Tying the Bridle Lines

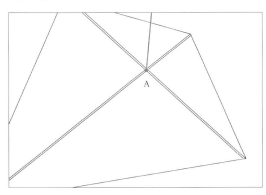

Tie string to point A using the "single-string connection" method explained before. Done.

2. Goldfish Kite

Fish is a symbol of wish fulfilment in Chinese culture, because fish (*yu*) is homophonous to surplus (*yu*). For the same reason, a fish dish is de rigueur on the table of every household in China on the lunar New Year's Day and paper cuts or paintings with fish motifs are a fixture in many Chinese households, representing aspirations for prosperity and wish fulfilment in the coming year.

This kite is a typical soft-paddle kite. The asterisk frame is in the shape of the Chinese character 米 and the painted sail features a green goldfish with big, fetching eyes.

Construction of the Frame

The frame of this kite is composed of a central spar, a wing edge and diagonal spars. Like the phoenix kite, which is also a soft-paddle kite, this kite has its frame put together with glue instead of with lashings.

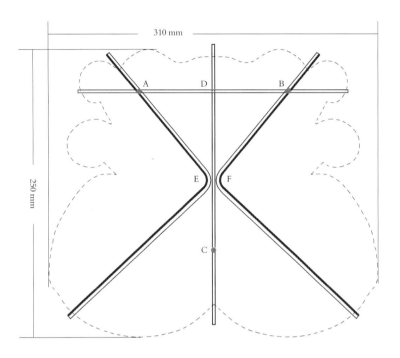

◼ Central spar: length 245 mm; upper width 2 mm, thickness 1.5 mm; lower width 1.5 mm, thickness 0.7 mm

═ The side view of the bamboo cross section

▦ Wing edge: length 255 mm; width 1.8 mm; thickness 3 mm

═ The inner surface of the bamboo facing up

--- Border of the painted sail

▦ Diagonal spars: length 340 mm; upper width 1 mm, thickness 2 mm; lower width 0.6 mm, thickness 1.5 mm

⬤ Point where a bridle line is attached to the frame

Making the Frame Components

Follow the dimensions and shape specified in the kite plan to make the wing edge, using the technique of "making a one-piece wing edge" explained before; make the central spar, using the technique of "making a central spar" explained before; make the diagonal spars, using the technique of "symmetrical splitting" explained before. The frame components are completed.

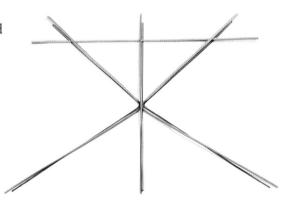

Painting the Sail

1 Use red, purple, yellow and black pigments to paint the eyes and gills; use black to delineate the contours.

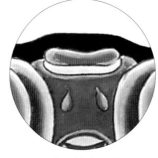

2 Use red and light yellow to paint the lips and nostrils.

3 Paint an ancient Chinese coin between the eyes with yellow and brown pigments.

4 Use green and yellow pigments for the pectoral and pelvic fins, and use black to delineate the contours.

5 Use green and yellow pigments to paint a squamous pattern on the body; use black to delineate the contours. Use light green and dark green pigments to paint the dorsal fins.

6 Use green and yellow pigments to paint the tail fins and use black to delineate the contours.

Assembling the Frame Components and Pasting the Sail

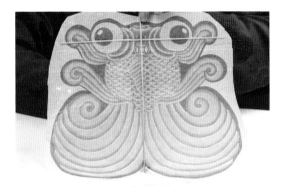

1 Glue the central spar and the wing edge together at right angles; then paste the painted sail onto the cruciform frame.

2 Glue the diagonal spars onto the painted sail, with one end of each diagonal spar overlapping the wing edge. Glue the diagonals to the wing edge; no lashing is necessary.

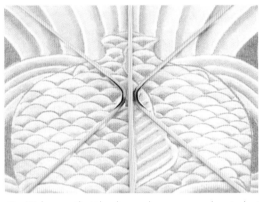

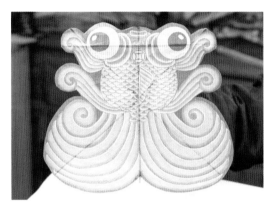

3 Make sure that the diagonal spars come close to but not in contact with the central spar.

4 After the pasting is done, trim the excess paper along the margin.

Tying the Bridle Lines

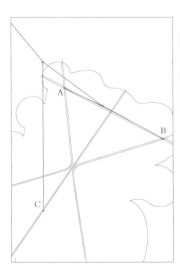

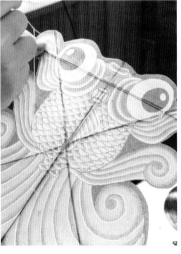

Attach the bridle lines at points A, B and C, using the "three-string connection" method explained before. Done.

3. Monkey King Facial Pattern Kite

The Monkey King is one of the main characters in *Journey to the West*, one of the Four Great Classical Novels of China. The Monkey King is known for supernatural powers, including the ability of seventy-two transformations. His help is indispensable in enabling Master Tripitaka (Master Xuanzang) of the Tang dynasty to successfully complete his journey to the west to procure true Scriptures. Beijing opera also draws on his story. Beijing opera boasts a rich variety of facial patterns; different colors and patterns represent distinct characters and personalities. The Monkey King's facial pattern features an inverted red peach with a silver lining, which symbolizes valor and chivalry.

This kite featuring a Monkey King mask is a typical soft-paddle kite; its frame is in the shape of an open umbrella. The painted sail depicts in bright colors the alert expression of the Monkey King. Like the phoenix kite, this kite has two tail streamers pasted to the underside of the painted sail to improve equilibrium.

Construction of the Frame

The frame of this kite assumes the shape of an umbrella, consisting of a central spar, a wing edge and two diagonal spars.

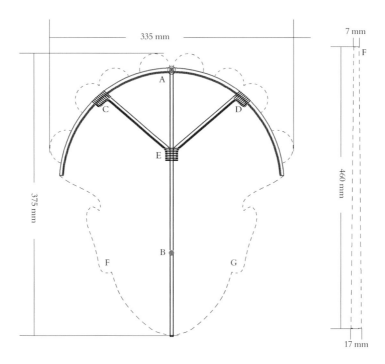

- ■ Central spar: length 350 mm; upper width 2 mm, thickness 1.5 mm; lower width 1.5 mm, thickness 0.7 mm
- ■ Diagonal spars: length 140 mm; upper width 1 mm, thickness 2 mm; lower width 0.6 mm, thickness 1.5 mm
- ═ The inner surface of the bamboo facing up
- ⊗ Diagonal lashing

- ▥ Wing edge: length 460 mm; thickness in the middle 3 mm, thickness at the two ends 2 mm; width 1.8 mm
- ═ The side view of the bamboo cross section
- --- Border of the painted sail   ║║║ Shear lashing
- ● Point where a bridle line is attached to the frame

Making the Frame Components

Follow the dimensions and shape specified in the kite plan to make the wing edge, using the technique of "making a one-piece wing edge"; make the central spar as explained before; make the diagonal spars using the "symmetrical splitting" technique explained before. The frame components are completed.

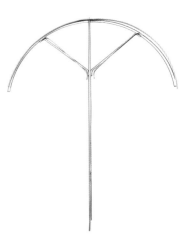

Assembling the Frame

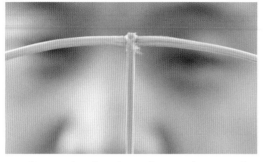

1 Connect the wing edge to the central spar at point A, using the "slit-end" method of assembling bamboo strips explained before and bind the two pieces together with a diagonal lashing.

2 Next, attach the diagonal spars to the wing edge and the central spar at points C, D and E, using the kneeling type attachment method explained before, and bind the pieces with shear lashings.

Painting the Sail

1 Use black, brown and blue pigments to paint the eyes, eyebrows and the rims of the eyes.

2 Use black and gray for the nose and the mouth; use red for the inverted peach in which the eyes and the mouth are imbedded.

3 Add a silver margin around the peach and an ornamental pattern in black and gray over the silver background.

4 Use orange, brown and black pigments to paint the cheeks, ears and the hair peeking out of his headdress.

5 Use yellow, red, blue, white, brown and black pigments to paint the headdress worn by the Monkey King.

6 Use black for the tail streamers hanging down from the headdress.

Pasting

1 Apply glue to the frame, paste the painted sail on the frame and cut off excess margin.

2 Paste the tail streamers to the underside of the painted sail just below the ears.

3 Done.

Tying the Bridle Lines

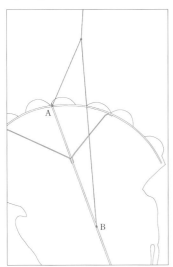

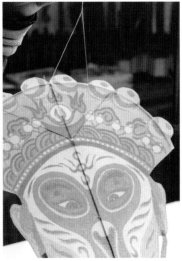

Tie the bridle lines to points A and B, using the "two-string connection" method explained before. Done.

4. Eight Trigrams Kite

Gua, divinatory trigrams, constitute a system of yin and yang that attempts to explain changes. At the center of the Eight Trigrams are two fish representing *taiji*, the white fish standing for yang and the black fish standing for yin. The symbol suggests the mutual inclusivity of yin and yang. Surrounding the circular center of yin and yang are eight trigrams composed of three lines each. The broken line "– –" represents yin and the unbroken line "—" represents yang.

The Eight Trigrams kite is a typical hard-paddle kite. Unlike the soft-paddle kites, its four sides are secured onto a rigid frame. Additionally this kite is ornamented by a colorful Y-shaped tail composed of 15 paper tassels, which plays a role in stabilizing the kite in flight.

Construction of the Frame

The frame is composed of two squares and a cross, including a central spar, a central cross spar and eight edge spars. A total of ten straight bamboo strips are needed for this kite frame. Make sure each square sub-frame stays on a plane.

The Y-shaped streamer of paper tassels is strung together with two strings. Each tassel is 100 mm high and the tassels are spaced 100 mm apart.

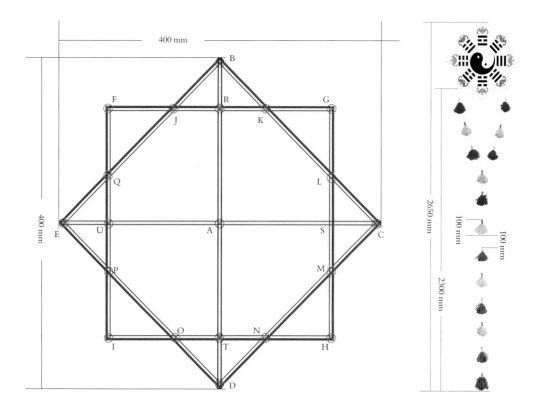

■ Central spar: length 400 mm; upper width 2 mm, thickness 1.5 mm; lower width 1.5 mm, thickness 0.7 mm

▓ Central cross spar: length 400 mm; width 1.8 mm; thickness in the middle 3 mm

▓ Edge spars: length 283 mm; upper width 1 mm, thickness 2 mm; lower width 0.6 mm, thickness 1.5 mm

▬ The side view of the bamboo cross section

═ The inner surface of the bamboo facing up

⊗ Diagonal lashing

● Point where a bridle line is attached to the frame

Making the Frame Components

Make ten straight bamboo strips, following the specs of the kite plan. Make sure the eight edge spars are uniform in width, thickness and flexibility. You may leave the lengths a little longer than in the specs to facilitate gluing and lashing.

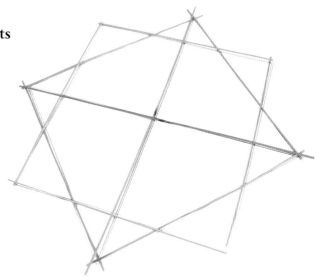

Assembling the Frame

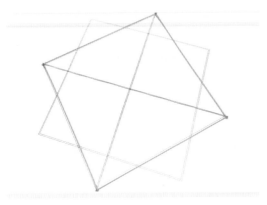

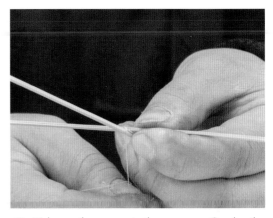

1 Make slits in both ends of four of the edge spars and assemble them into a square, using the "double slit-end" connection method explained earlier; glue the connections and bind them with diagonal lashings.

2 Make another square in the same way. Overlap the two squares following the kite plan at points J, K, L, M, N, O, P and Q; bind the two squares at those points of intersection with diagonal lashings.

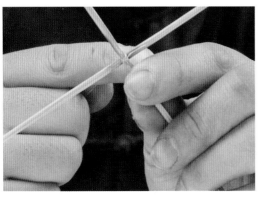

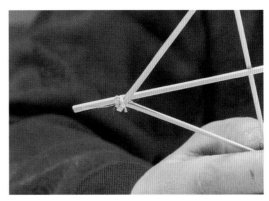

3 Assemble the central spar and the central cross spar into a cross, using the "overlap" connection method, and bind them together with a diagonal lashing.

4 Superimpose the cross-shaped sub-frame with the two square sub-frames, using the "overlap" connection method, and bind them together with diagonal lashings.

5 Apply superglue to all connections to make them more robust. After the glue sets, use side-cutting pliers to remove excess bamboo.

6 The frame is completed.

Painting the Sail

1 Paint a *taiji* yin-yang diagram in the center of the sail with black ink.

2 Paint eight trigrams around the yin-yang diagram.

3 At the four corners corresponding to one square sub-frame, paint four green bats like this.

4 Paint four red bats like this at the four corners corresponding to the other square sub-frame.

Pasting

1 Apply glue to the frame and paste the painted sail onto the frame. Cut off excess paper but leave enough margin for gluing around the edge.

2 All the components of the Eight Trigrams kite being straight bamboo strips, the margin can be directly glued down around the edge.

3 The pasting is completed.

Making the Long Tail of Paper Tassels

1 Take a 10 cm by 20 cm piece of red crepe paper, fold it four or five times over itself and cut strips at the lower end to create a fringe.

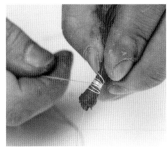

2 Roll the tassel tightly around a string, and lash another string around the wrapping.

3 Take a 3 cm by 5 cm piece of yellow crepe paper and wrap it around the head of the tassel and glue it down, hiding the lashing.

4 One paper tassel is created. Make a total of 15 tassels and string them up into a Y-shaped streamer, alternating tassels of different colors.

Tying the Bridle Lines

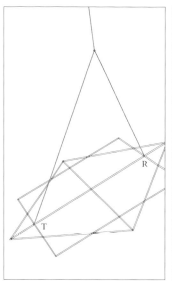

Tie the bridle lines at points R and T, using the "two-string connection" method.

Puncture a small hole in the painted sail at points I and H and thread the paper tassel lines through the respective holes and tie them to the bamboo strips. The kite is completed.

5. Eagle Kite

This is a typical soft-wing kite. It is said to be single-layer because there is only one pair of wings to it. It is called "soft-wing" because only the upper edge of the wings is attached to a rigid strip while the lower edge is left free. Due to its huge wing span, powerful claws and sharp eyes, the eagle is a symbol of freedom, power and valor. The grace and power of an eagle kite are shown to advantage when it flies in the blue sky.

Construction of the Frame

The central spar is uppermost; after the wing edge and the diagonal spar are attached to the central spar, the wing loops and the wing edge will be on the same plane, the tail spar and the central spar are also on the same plane. There is no 3-D construction, with everything basically on the same plane. Make sure the surface of the side of the frame onto which the painted sail is to be glued is smooth.

During the construction of the individual components, note that due to the fact that trimming of the bamboo strips is done only on the top and bottom surfaces but not on the sides, the bamboo fibers may still bend sideways and therefore it may be necessary after the spars are cut to the final thickness and width to correct sideway curvatures by heating the components as appropriate.

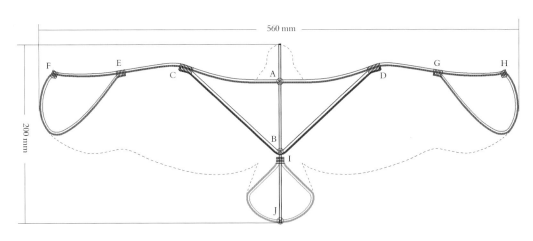

■ Central spar: length 200 mm; upper width 1.8 mm, thickness 1.5 mm; lower width 1 mm, thickness 0.7 mm

▓ Wing edge: length 540 mm; middle width 2 mm, thickness in the middle 3 mm; tip width 1 mm, thickness 1 mm

▓ Diagonal spar: length 310 mm; width 1.2 mm; thickness 1 mm

▓ Wing loops: length 200 mm; thickness 1 mm; width 1 mm

▓ Tail spar: length 220 mm; width 0.5 mm; thickness 0.8 mm

═ The inner surface of the bamboo facing up

▬ The side view of the bamboo cross section

--- Border of the painted sail

⊗ Diagonal lashing

||||| Shear lashing

● Point where a bridle line is attached to the frame

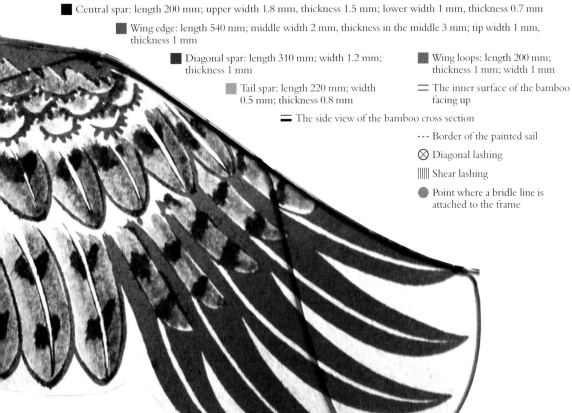

Making the Frame Components

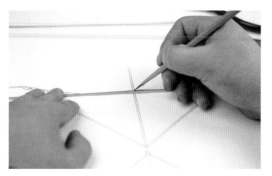

1 Draw a kite plan to scale on paper.

2 Making the central spar: In order to meet the requirement of a rigid leading edge and a soft trailing edge, the central spar needs to taper from front to rear in both width and thickness. When making the central spar, constantly test its rigidity and flexibility and adjust as needed until it satisfies the requirement.

3 Making the wing edge: To meet the requirement of a rigid middle and more flexible ends, the wing edge must taper from the middle outward in width and thickness. When making it, constantly test its rigidity and adjust as needed until the same rigidity is achieved at the right and the left end.

4 Heat the wing edge until its curvature matches the specs of the kite plan.

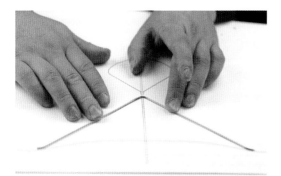

5 Making the diagonal spar: The diagonal spar is of uniform width and thickness throughout its length. Place the spar with the bamboo pulp facing up and the bamboo skin facing down.

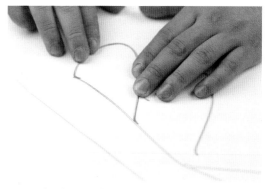

6 Make the wing loops using the symmetrical split technique. The wing loops should have uniform width and thickness. Place the loops with the bamboo pulp facing up and the bamboo skin facing down.

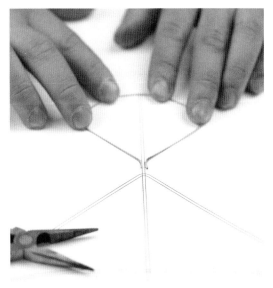

7 Making the tail spar: The tail spar has uniform width and thickness. Place it with the bamboo skin facing up and the bamboo pulp facing down.

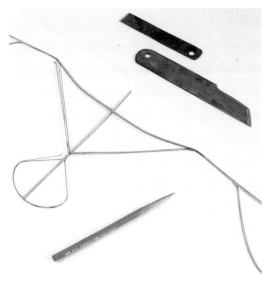

8 The making of the components is now complete.

Assembling the Frame

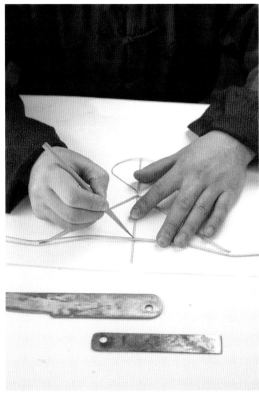

1 As illustrated in the kite plan, mark with a pencil the points of attachment on all components.

2 Using the diagonal lashing technique, tie the central spar and the wing edge together at point A.

3 Using the diagonal lashing technique, attach the center of the diagonal spar to the central spar at point B; using the shear lashing technique, attach the diagonal spar to the wing edge by kneeling type attachment at points C and D (the diagonal spar is under the central spar).

4 Tie the two wing loops with shear lashing to the wing edge at points E, F and G, H by using kneeling type attachment (so that the loops are under the wing edge).

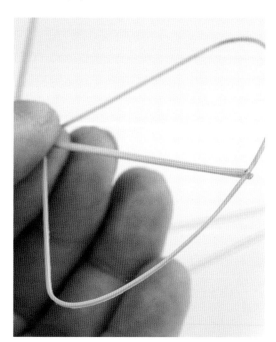

5 Heat-treat the tail section ends and tie them with shear lashing technique to the central spar at point I by using kneeling type attachment, then using the diagonal lashing, fit the tail spar into the slit end of the central spar at point J with the slit-end attachment.

6 After all components are attached, test to see if the flexibility of the left side of the assembled frame equals that of the right; adjust as appropriate. The assembly of the frame is now complete.

Painting the Sail

1 Paint the eagle head in brown, the eyes in black and purple with the centers left blank.

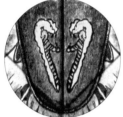

2 Paint the eagle claws in yellow.

3 Paint the feathers in brown.

4 Add black dots to the brown feathers and allow the ink to ooze outward.

Pasting

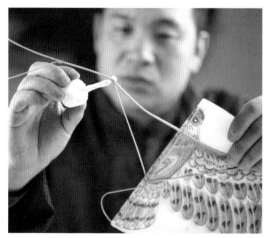

1 Apply glue to the wing edge at the two ends, the wing loops and the tail spar.

2 Apply glue to the central spar.

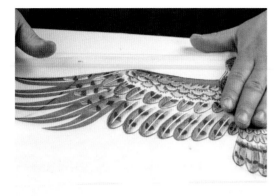

3 Glue the eagle wings to the frame and smooth it down.

4 Glue the central spar to the backside of the painted sail.

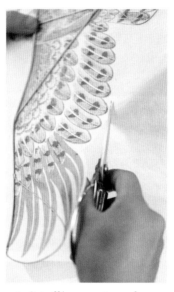

5 Smooth the painted sail over the central spar from the front side.

6 Cut off large sections of excess blank paper to facilitate later trimming of the edges.

7 Leave narrow flaps of paper for wrapping around the spars and cut off excess paper.

8 Apply glue all around the wrapping spots and glue the paper strips down securely.

9 Done.

Tying the Bridle Lines

1 Tie the bridle line with a diagonal lashing around the intersection of the central spar and the wing edge at point A.

2 Then tie the bridle line with a diagonal lashing around the intersection of the central spar and the diagonal spar at point B. Make sure the bridle line measures 11 cm between points A and B, longer than the distance between the two points.

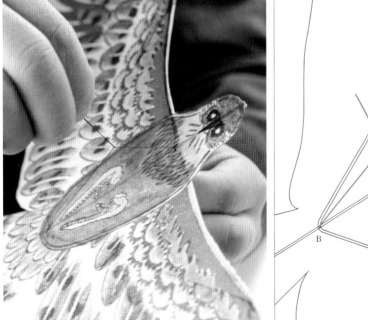

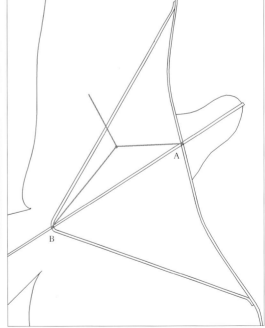

3 Find the center of gravity on the bridle line between points A and B and make a loop with the eye knot at the point for connecting the flying line.

6. Butterfly Kite

Butterflies are colorful, beautiful creatures; they flit about like merry fairies. In Chinese culture, butterflies are a symbol of romantic love. In *Liang Shanbo and Zhu Yingtai*, also known as *The Butterfly Lovers*, a romantic love story no less moving than *Romeo and Juliet*, the two lovers in the end turn into a pair of butterflies and fly away together.

This butterfly kite is a typical multiple-layer soft-wing kite. It is called multiple-layer because it has two pairs of wings and it is called soft-wing because the wings are rigid at the front or upper edges while remaining flexible at the bottom edges.

Construction of the Frame

The frame of this kite is composed of a central spar, two main wing edges and one second-tier wing edge.

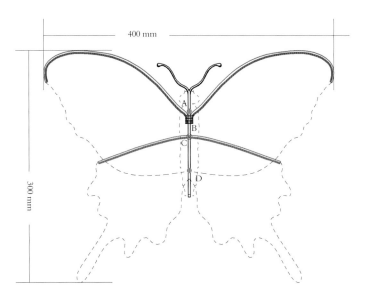

■ Central spar (including the antennae): length 200 mm; upper width 2 mm, thickness 1.5 mm; lower width 1.5 mm, thickness 0.7 mm

▦ Second-tier wing edge: length 260 mm; upper width 1 mm, thickness 2 mm; lower width 0.6 mm, thickness 1.5 mm

⊗ Diagonal lashing

▥ Shear lashing

▦ Main wing edges: length 240 mm; width in the middle 1.8 mm; thickness 3 mm

▬ The side view of the bamboo cross section

═ The inner surface of the bamboo facing up

--- Border of the painted sail

● Point where a bridle line is attached to the frame

Making the Frame Components

1 Make the central spar as explained before. The antennae take some work. At a point of the central spar about 10 mm from its top end, shave the bamboo pulp in the direction of the lower end.

2 Leave the top of the spar thicker than the rest of it. The side view of the spar will show a protuberance at the top. Polish the protuberance at the top.

3 The picture shows the result of polishing.

4 Shave and scrape the central spar in such a way that the antennae are thick and rigid at the base and thin and flexible at the top; the main part of the central spar should be rigid and thick in the middle and thinner and more flexible at the two ends.

5 Heat the top of the central spar corresponding to the antennae.

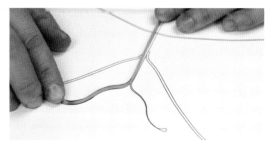

6 Bend the antenna part of the central spar to the curvature specified in the kite plan.

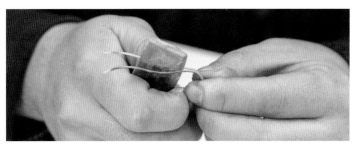

7 After the spar is heat-bent to shape, split the top of the central spar to form the two feelers, using the "symmetrical splitting" technique explained before.

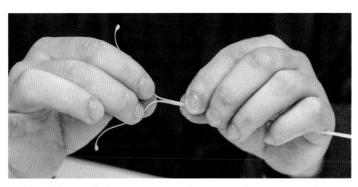

8 Bend the two feelers to opposite sides at an angle to the central spar.

9 The central spar is completed.

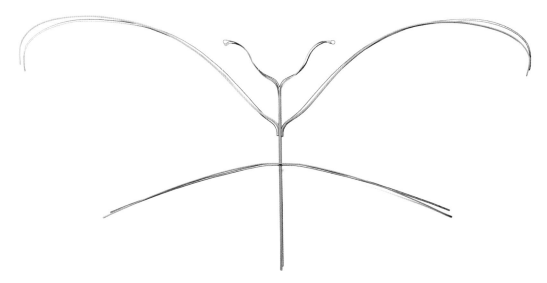

10 Make the main wing edges using the "symmetrical splitting" technique explained before; make the second-tier wing edge using "making a one-piece wing edge" technique explained before.

Assembling the Frame

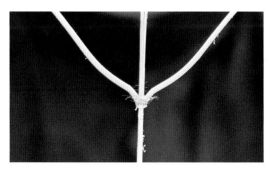

1 Connect the two main wing edges to the central spar, using the kneeling type attachment, and bind them together with shear lashings.

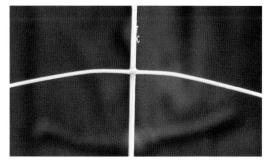

2 Connect the second-tier wing edge to the central spar in the "overlap" fashion and bind them together with diagonal lashings.

3 After the frame is assembled, the main wing edges may present unsymmetrical flexibility at the two sides due to slight differences in the lashings.

4 In this case, make fine adjustments by shaving and scraping until left-right symmetry in flexibility is achieved.

Painting the Sail

The butterfly kite has three painted sails: the upper wings, the lower wings and the torso including the head. They are painted separately.

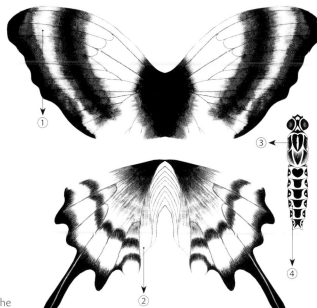

1 Use blue, black and green pigments to paint the upper wings.

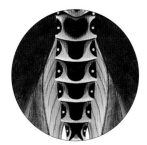

2 Use blue, black, green, yellow and red pigments to paint the lower wings.

3 Use black, red and yellow pigments to paint the head and the thorax.

4 Use peach red, yellow and black pigments to paint the abdomen.

Pasting

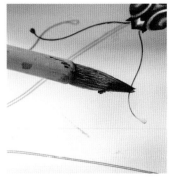

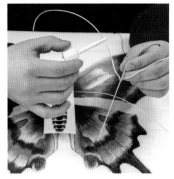

1 Use black ink to paint the antennae.

2 Apply glue to the main wing edges and the top part of the central spar.

3 Paste the painted upper wings to the main wing edges and the upper part of the central spar.

4 Cut the bottom of the upper-wings painted sail in the middle to point C.

5 The second-tier wing edge and the lower half of the central spar are thus exposed.

6 Apply glue to the second-tier wing edge and the lower part of the central spar.

7 Cut off excess paper around the lower-wings painted sail.

8 Paste the lower-wings painted sail to the frame.

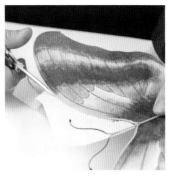

9 Trim around the edge.

10 Cut out the torso, including the head, the thorax and the abdomen.

11 Paste the torso painted sail between the wings, as shown.

12 The pasting is done.

Tying the Bridle Lines

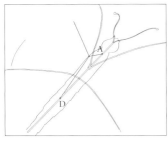

Follow the kite plan to attach the bridle lines to points A and D, using the "two-string connection" method explained before. Done.

7. Petty Official Kite

This picture of a petty official is drawn from a character in Chinese folk opera. The seventh-rank petty official holds in his hands a shoe-shaped gold ingot and rides on an auspicious symbol bearing the Chinese ideogram (*fu*, good fortune) against a background of bats and auspicious cloud patterns, both of which suggest good luck.

This is a typical asterisk-frame hard-wing kite. The frame is in the shape of the Chinese character 米 and the kite is categorized as hard-wing because the frame consists of a fixed wing edge both along its upper and lower edges.

Construction of the Frame

The frame of this kite is composed of a central spar, an upper wing edge, a lower wing edge, two diagonal spars and a secondary spar. The central spar and the two diagonal spars are on one plane and are positioned in the back; the upper and lower wing edges are on one plane, positioned in front. The curvature of the upper and lower wing edges in this hard-wing kite is not formed by heating the bamboo strips but rather by the tension created when they are bound together. The upper and lower wing edges are connected to form a closed wing-shaped structure, which together with the painted sail creates a wind pocket that both captures and passes through wind.

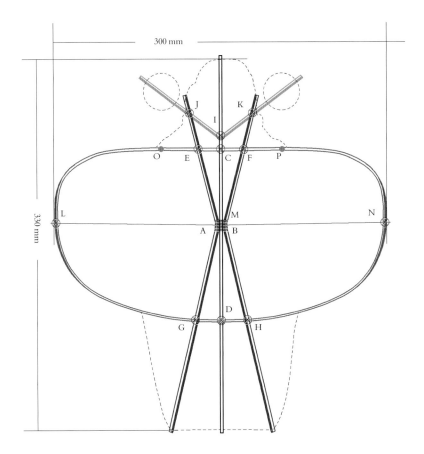

■ Central spar: length 330 mm; upper width 2 mm, thickness 1.5 mm; lower width 1.5 mm, thickness 0.7 mm

▨ Lower wing edge: length 370 mm; width in the middle 1.2 mm, thickness 1.5 mm; width at the two ends 0.8 mm, thickness 0.4 mm

▨ Secondary spar: length 170 mm; width 1 mm; thickness 1 mm

⚌ The inner surface of the bamboo facing up

⊗ Diagonal lashing   ‖‖‖ Shear lashing

▨ Upper wing edge: length 370 mm; width in the middle 1.8 mm, thickness 2 mm; width at the two ends 1 mm, thickness 0.5 mm

■ Diagonal spars: length 300 mm; width in the middle 1.5 mm, thickness 2 mm; width at the two ends 1 mm, thickness 1 mm

⚌ The side view of the bamboo cross section

— Transverse string   --- Border of the painted sail

● Point where a bridle line is attached to the frame

Making the Frame Components

1 Make the central spar as explained before. Adjust the central spar so that it is rigid in the upper part and becomes more flexible toward the lower part.

2 Make the upper wing edge using "making a one-piece wing edge" technique. Adjusting the upper wing edge to make sure there is left-right symmetry and that the middle section is rigid enough to allow bending to desired shape called for by the kite plan.

3 Making the lower wing edge using the same method as that of the upper wing edge. Adjust the lower wing edge to ensure there is left-right symmetry and that it is more flexible than the upper wing edge and allows for greater bendability.

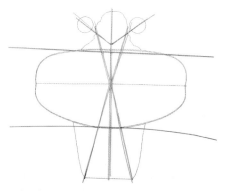

4 Make the secondary spar using "making a one-piece wing edge" technique. Make two symmetrical diagonal spars using the "symmetrical splitting" technique. When making the components in the rough, make sure to leave extra lengths to allow for future adjustments.

Assembling the Frame

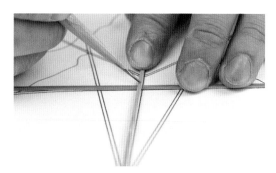

1 Mark with a pencil points where the various components are to be connected.

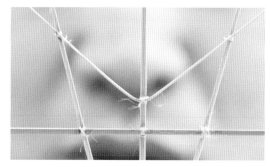

2 Connect the central spar, the upper and lower wing edges using the overlap attachment explained before and bind them with diagonal lashings.

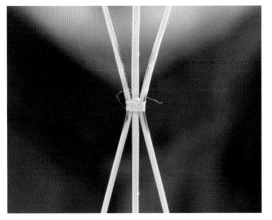

3 Connect the diagonal spars to the central spar using the kneeling type attachment explained before and bind them with shear lashings.

4 Connect the diagonal spars to the secondary spar, the upper and the lower wing edges using the overlap attachment and bind them with diagonal lashings.

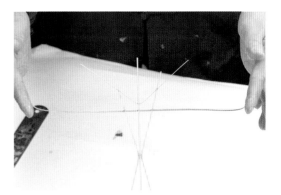

5 The picture shows the result after the rough components of the frame are assembled.

6 Next make the wing pocket. After the preliminary assembly of the frame, slight differences in the lashings could lead to loss of left-right symmetry and therefore it may be necessary to readjust the wing edges. Bend the upper and lower wing edges to the shapes specified in the kite plan; adjust as appropriate.

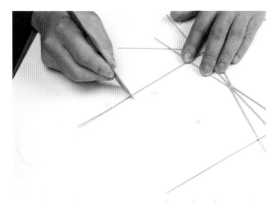

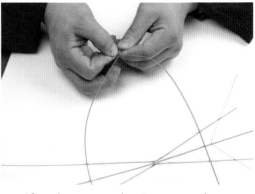

7 Where there is excessive rigidity, adjust by scraping the bamboo strip to make it thinner until the desired flexibility is achieved.

8 After adjustments and testing, connect the upper and lower wing edges.

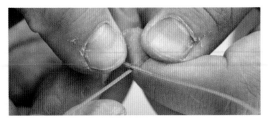

9 Connect the upper and lower wing edges at one end using the overlap attachment, with the upper wing edge on top of the lower, and secure them with a diagonal lashing but do not tie a knot at this stage.

10 Draw the string used to lash the connection across to where the central spar and the diagonal spars intersect in the center of the frame, making sure that the length of the string matches the specification in the kite plan.

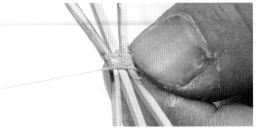

11 Secure the string to points A and B by wrapping a turn around the intersection.

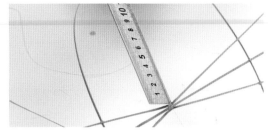

12 Continue to draw the string across to the point on the other side where the upper and lower wing edges are to be connected; make sure with a straight edge that the length of the string matches the kite plan specs.

13 Then connect the upper and lower wing edges, with the upper wing edge on top of the lower, and secure the connection with a diagonal lashing.

14 The assembly of the frame is complete.

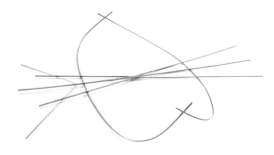

15 Viewed from the side, the frame is not on one plane.

16 The wing pocket is shaped by the tension in the connected upper and lower wing edges and this tension could distort the kite frame before the glue on the various components dries completely. To prevent this distortion, it is necessary to keep a weight over the central section of the frame for about 12 hours.

Painting the Sail

There are five separate pieces to the painted sail of the petty official kite: the head, the left arm, the right arm, the legs and the wing-like flaps on the hat. They are painted separately. Make sure they match each other seamlessly when put together.

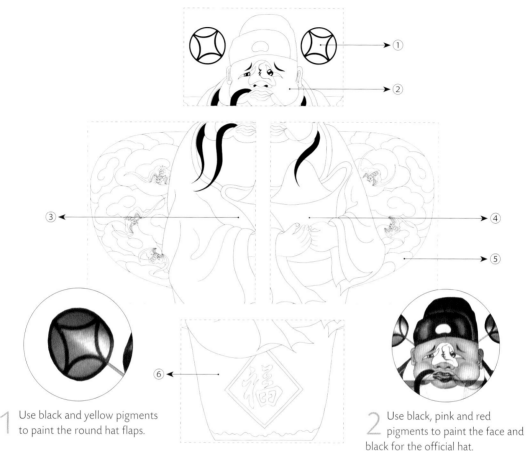

1 Use black and yellow pigments to paint the round hat flaps.

2 Use black, pink and red pigments to paint the face and black for the official hat.

3 Paint the right half body first. Use black pigment to delineate the outlines and red to paint the robe, green to paint the cuff of the sleeve and yellow to paint the shoe-shaped gold ingot.

4 Next paint the left half. Use black pigment to delineate the outlines, red for the robe, pink for the hands, green for the sleeve cuff and yellow for the gold ingot.

5 Paint blue cloud patterns on the background and add bats in green, purple and red.

6 Lastly paint the lower part of the petty official. Use brown pigment to paint the lower official garment; add the Chinese character 福 in yellow against a red backdrop with a blue border.

Pasting

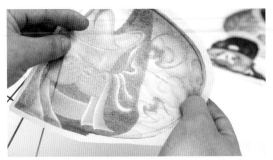 

1 Start by pasting the right arm. Place the painted piece against the frame and mark with a pencil the points at which the string strung across the wing pocket meets the two sides of the painted piece.

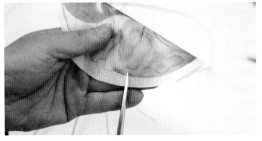 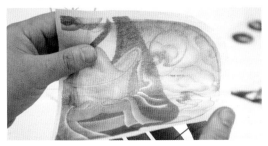

2 Cut a small notch at the two marked points.

3 Place the painted piece back over the frame and make sure the transverse string is pressed against the painted sail.

 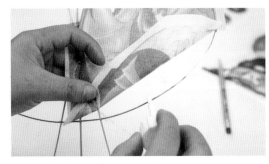

4 Apply glue to the central spar and the diagonal spars.

5 Apply glue to the wing pocket.

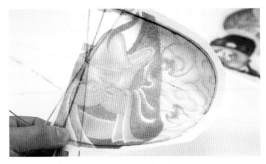 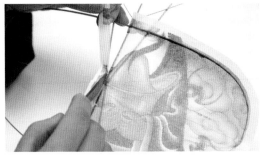

6 Paste the painted piece to the frame.

7 Trim excess paper next to the central spar.

8 Do the same with the left arm.

9 Trim around the edge.

10 Apply glue to the part of the frame corresponding to the official's head.

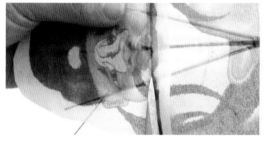

11 Paste the painted head piece to the frame and trim the edge.

12 Paste the painted hat flaps to the two ends of the secondary spar.

13 Lastly paste the lower painted piece to the frame. Done.

Tying the Bridle Lines

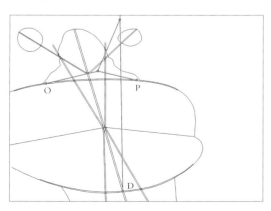

Tie the bridle lines to points O, P and D, using the "three-string connection" method explained before. The kite is completed.

8. Good Fortune and Longevity Swallow Kite

Swallows are migratory birds that fly south to winter as soon as the first cold wave hits. In Chinese folk belief it is a sign of good fortune when a swallow makes a nest in one's house. The painted sail of a swallow kite assumes the general shape of a swallow, beautifully ornamented by auspicious symbols such as fish, bats and *ruyi*, etc.

The swallow kite is a typical hard-wing kite. It consists of a head, two wings, two tails and the torso, which together assume the shape of the Chinese character 大 (which means "big").

Construction of the Frame

The frame of this kite is composed of a body frame in the shape of an inverted U, an upper wing edge, a lower wing edge, two tail spars, a pair of upper ornamental corners and a pair of lower ornamental corners. The two tail spars are on the same plane and are placed in the back of all other frame components.

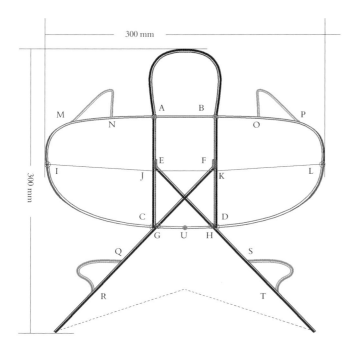

Body frame: length 360 mm; width 1 mm, thickness 2 mm

Upper wing edge: length 360 mm; width in the middle 1.8 mm, thickness 2 mm; width at the two ends 1 mm, thickness 0.5 mm

Lower wing edge: length 360 mm; width in the middle 1.2 mm, thickness 1.5 mm; width at the two ends 0.8 mm, thickness 0.4 mm

Tail spars: length 250 mm; upper width 1 mm, thickness 2 mm; lower width 1 mm, thickness 1.5 mm

Ornamental corners: length 90 mm; width 1 mm; thickness 1 mm

The side view of the bamboo cross section

The inner surface of the bamboo facing up

Transverse string

Border of the painted sail

⊗ Diagonal lashing

|||| Shear lashing

● Point where a bridle line is attached to the frame

Making the Frame Components

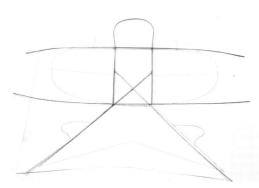

1 Make the upper wing edge, the lower wing edge and the body frame using the "making a one-piece wing edge" technique explained before; make the tail spars using the "symmetrical splitting" technique.

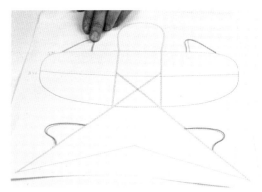

2 Make the four ornamental spars, using the "symmetrical splitting" technique, making sure of left-right symmetry.

Assembling the Frame

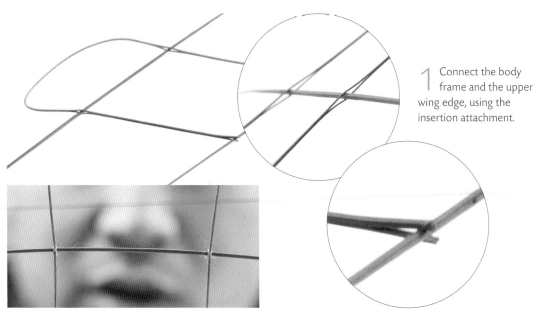

1 Connect the body frame and the upper wing edge, using the insertion attachment.

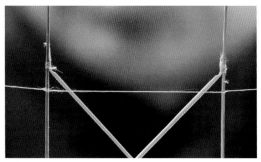

2 And secure the body frame and the upper wing edge with diagonal lashings.

3 Connect the body frame to the lower wing edge, using the slit-end attachment, and secure with diagonal lashings.

4 Connect the tail spars to the inside of the body frame, using the kneeling type attachment, and secure with shear lashings.

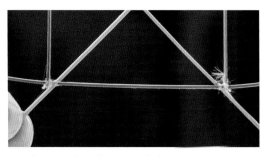

5 Connect the tail spars to the lower wing edge, using the overlap attachment, and secure with diagonal lashings.

6 Make the wing pocket of this swallow kite, following the steps in making the wing pocket for the petty official kite by connecting the upper and lower wing edges.

Painting the Sail

The painted sail of the good fortune and longevity swallow kite consists of five parts: the body consisting of the head, the thorax and the abdomen, two wings and two tails.

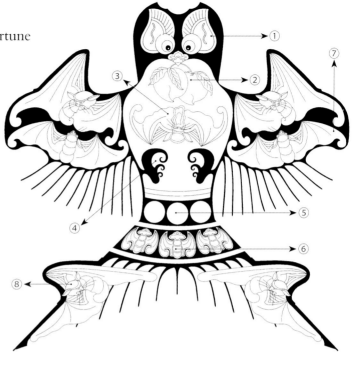

1 Use yellow, red, black, blue, pink, green and brown pigments to paint the head of the swallow.

2 Use yellow, red and green pigments to paint the two peaches hanging from the swallow's beak.

3 Use red, yellow and green pigments to paint a bat on the chest of the swallow .

4 Use black to paint the swallow's claws.

5 Use red, black and yellow pigments to paint the abdomen.

6 Then use blue and white pigments to paint three bats on the abdomen.

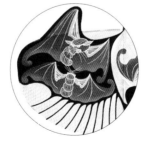

7 Use red, yellow, blue and green pigments to paint the bats on the two wings; then pen in the ornamental lines in black.

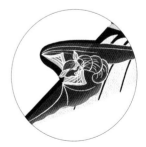

8 Use red, yellow, blue and green pigments to paint the bats on the tails; then pen in the ornamental lines in black.

Pasting

1 Before pasting the painted pieces, bend the two tails slightly outward to ensure the sail is spread taut and nice over them.

2 First paste the painted pieces of the body and the head on the frame.

3 Apply glue on the tail spars.

4 Paste the painted piece for the tail on the frame.

5 Press down on the painted pieces and stretch them taut over the frame.

6 Cut small notches (to the edge of the frame) in the painted pieces where the head meets the wings, and where the tails meet the lower edge of the wings; this is to facilitate later pasting.

7 Apply glue to the wing edges and paste the painted wings to the frame.

8 The pasting of the painted wings, head and tails is completed.

9 Trim the edge around all painted pieces, except where the ornamental corners are to be attached.

10 Apply glue on the ornamental corners and match them with the painted sail.

11 Keep a weight on the ornamental corner while applying glue to the points at which the corner is attached to the wing edge to make the connection more secure. After the glue dries, trim around the edge of the ornamental corner.

12 The swallow kite is completed.

Tying the Bridle Lines

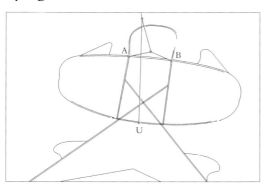

Tie the bridle lines to points A, B and U, using the "three-string connection" method explained before. The kite is completed.

Fig. 96 *Dragon Kite Train* by Zhi Ruili
Kite train
Dragon kite trains are composed of a dragon's head and a dragon's body. The head is mainly decorative and cannot fly by itself; the body is made up of multiple identical sections, each of which is independently flyable.

CHAPTER 5
HOW TO FLY A KITE

The ability to fly is the soul of a kite. A kite has meaning only when it is able to fly. If a kite can't fly, it cannot properly be called a kite, no matter how clever the design, how exquisite the craftsmanship and how pretty the painted sail is. At rest, a kite is not much different from a bird painting or a stuffed bird. It is in flight that a kite comes to life and deploys all its charms. Flying a kite takes a certain amount of knowledge, experience and skill.

1. Getting Ready

Before you can fly your kite, you need wind. Kite flying can be done in any wide open space with enough wind; location, weather and wind conditions are important considerations to ensure a satisfying experience in flying your kites.

Location

Launching the kite is the first step in kite flying. Winds can be quite fickle close to the ground, and since you launch your kite near ground level, air turbulence could cause the kite to crash. Therefore it is important to choose a suitable location for launching.

Pick a location where air turbulence is minimal. Uneven terrain and obstacles close to the ground affect wind directions and speed near ground level. In a level, open field, wind speed and direction are relatively stable and kites are less likely to be snagged by obstacles and suffer damages. Bodies of water, such as lakes and ponds, have an open and level surface but are unsuitable for kite flying, for kites will be damaged when they come into contact with water. Plastic kites however can be flown over water.

Should you pick an upwind or downwind spot? If the wind speed is less than what's required to get a kite airborne, then you should choose a downwind location to launch your kite, for this will allow for a longer distance to run with the kite. If the wind is strong and the wind speed is greater than what's required for kite flight, then choose an upwind location for launching, so that you can decrease the speed of the kite by letting out line or running toward it (FIG. 97).

Wind direction

Upwind spot

Spot

Downwind spot

FIG. 97
The kite flier chooses an upwind or a downwind location, depending on the wind speed.

Weather

Do not fly kites in a thunder storm or when it rains to avoid electrocution.

Do not fly kites in a wind storm, including typhoons. If you do, you run the risk of having your kite blown away or yourself getting hurt.

Tip: It Is a Bad Idea to Fly Kites

- Close to highways or railroad tracks
- Close to landmarks or cultural heritage sites
- Close to airports or power lines

Wind

Different kites need different wind speeds for launching. You can make a reasonable judgment about wind direction and force and changes by referring to the Beaufort scale on the next page, which lists the winds effects for different wind forces and speeds.

Assess the wind force and wind speed for different altitudes. Wind force varies with altitude. Normally wind force is greater at higher altitudes (FIG. 98). Closer to ground, obstacles create turbulence and therefore kites are more difficult to control at lower altitudes; at higher altitudes, wind force and direction become more stable.

Launch your kite only when wind directions are stable; if wind is fickle, wait until it stabilizes before launching. Even the best kite will not be immune to crashing if it encounters turbulence during launch.

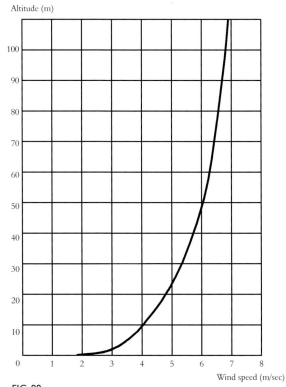

FIG. 98
This is a wind speed/altitude curve provided by a meteorological station. It shows how the wind speed varies with changing altitude.

Wind Force	Wind Speed (m/sec)	Appearance of Wind Effects
0	0–0.2	Calm, smoke rises vertically
1	0.3–1.5	Smoke drift indicates wind direction, still wind vanes
2	1.6–3.3	Wind felt on face, leaves rustle, vanes begin to move
3	3.4–5.4	Leaves and small twigs constantly moving, light flags extended
4	5.5–7.9	Dust, leaves, and loose paper lifted, small tree branches move
5	8.0–10.7	Small trees in leaf begin to sway, moderate waves
6	10.8–13.8	Larger tree branches moving, whistling in wires, difficulty in opening umbrellas
7	13.9–17.1	Whole trees moving, large tree branches bend low, resistance felt walking against wind
8	17.2–20.7	Twigs breaking off trees, generally impedes progress
9	20.8–24.4	Chimneys and roof damage occurs, smaller houses may suffer heavy damage
10	24.5–28.4	Seldom experienced on land, trees broken or uprooted
11	28.5–32.6	Rare on land, "considerable structural damage"
12	more than 32.6	Extremely rare on land, very destructive

Calculating the "Wing Load" of a Kite

The wind force appropriate for kite launching is not simply proportional to the kite's weight or mass. The view that bigger or heavier kites need a greater wind speed to launch is incorrect.

Here we will introduce the concept of wing load. Generally speaking, regardless of the size or weight of a kite, the greater the kite's wing load is, the greater the wind speed required for launch.

The "wing load" of a kite is the weight divided by the projected area of the kite. The projected area of a kite is the area of the shadow projected by it when placed directly under a light. The projected area of a flat kite is easily calculated: it is the area of the sail. With a 3-D or box kite, the area of its windward surface can be estimated based on the projected area.

For example: a diamond kite with a projected area of 26.06 square decimeters and a weight of 55 grams has a wing load of $55/26.06 = 2.11$ g/dm^2. A fan-shaped kite with a projected area of 14.08 dm^2, which is much smaller than the diamond kite mentioned before, and a weight of 35 g has a wing load of $35/14.08 = 2.49$ g/dm^2. As can be seen, a smaller kite doesn't necessarily have a smaller wing load; nor is the wing load of a bigger kite necessarily greater.

FIG. 99   *Dragon Kite* by Liu Bin
Paddle kite
A rhombus kite depicting a dragon going through auspicious clouds flies in the sky.

Kite Type, Wind Force, Wing Load Must All Be Taken into Account when Choosing the Right Conditions for Launching

We've created a chart showing the relationship between the required wind speed for launch and the wing load of three common types of kites: the soft-wing, the hard-wing and the paddle kites (FIG. 100). When we know the type of kite and its wing load, we can calculate from the curves in this chart the minimum required wind speed to maintain the kite in the air.

For example: for a diamond kite with a wing load of 2.1 g/dm^2, we locate on the X-axis, which represents the wing load, the point corresponding to 2.1 g/dm^2, draw a vertical line up from there; from the intersection of this vertical line with the curve for paddle kites, we draw a horizontal line and obtain the minimum required wind speed 3.9 m/sec at the intersection of that horizontal line with the Y-axis.

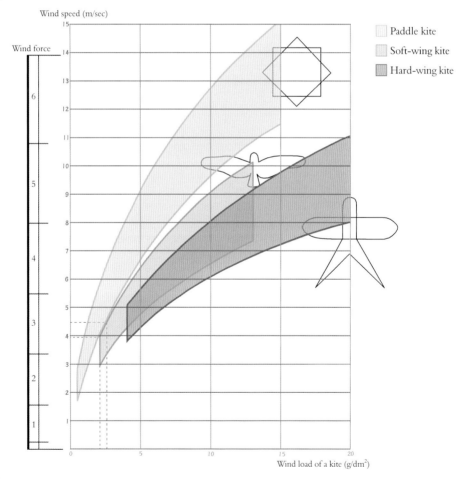

FIG. 100
Three curves showing, respectively for paddle, soft-wing and hard-wing kites, the relationship between kite type, wing load and wind speed suitable for launch

2. Launching, Flying and Flight Control

Here you will learn the skills to launch the kites, make them rise and control their flight.

Launching

With smaller kites, stand with your back to the wind, hold the kite, tug the line back and upwards to launch the kite. Once it is airborne, keep adjusting your posture as you let out line and the kite will start to rise (FIG. 102). Due to the turbulences that could be generated around your body, the kite may become unstable and even dive. Therefore you want to minimize such turbulences by slightly facing sideways to reduce the windward area of your body and limit the effect of the turbulences. When the kite rises, these turbulences will lose their effect on it.

FIG. 102
Smaller kites can be launched by one person.

It is relatively hard for one person to fly a large kite; in the circumstance you need an assistant to hold the kite at a downwind location. The person who holds the winder will let out a dozen or dozens of meters of line and wait upwind. When a good wind rises, the assistant will hold high the kite and release it, with the person holding the winder pulling on the flying line to make the kite rise (FIG. 103).

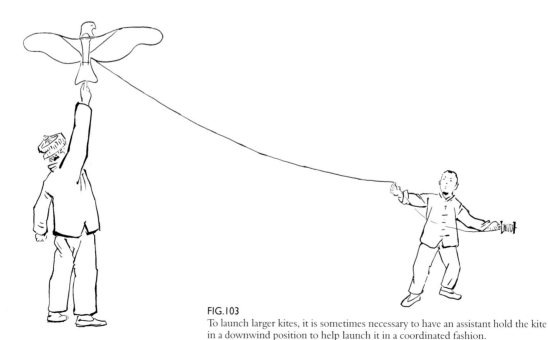

FIG.103
To launch larger kites, it is sometimes necessary to have an assistant hold the kite in a downwind position to help launch it in a coordinated fashion.

Gaining Altitude

Once the kite is launched, try to make it rise as soon as possible to a suitable altitude, for wind speed and direction are more stable at higher altitudes than near ground level and the kite will have an easier time staying in the air. There are several ways to make the kite gain altitude.

Standing: Ideally the kite flier should be able to launch the kite simply by deftly letting out and pulling in the flying line to manipulate the kite into flight without having to move about. That presupposes a good wind; it is doable when the wind speed reaches the minimum required for launch as shown in the wind speed/wing load chart. An experienced kite flier can launch the kite without moving about even at 70–80% of minimum required wind speed.

FIG. 101
A man is flying a modern kite.

Running: Run with your body turned sideways, with the winder in one hand and the flying line in the other, and keep your eyes on the kite behind you. Never run with your eyes on the ground and not on the kite; and never run backwards with your eyes on the kite. Adjust your running speed to the rise of the kite and the pull of the flying line on your hand: when the rise is slow and the pull is weak, run at a faster speed; when the kite is rising fast and the line pull is strong, you need to slow down; when the kite loses its balance and is in danger of diving, you should immediately let out line and stop running to wait for the kite to self-adjust and rise again.

Also, let out line at a suitable rate during the ascent of the kite. If you let out line too fast, the kite may not launch; if you let out line too slow, the kite may not reach a suitable altitude. Let out line so that the kite maintains a steady rate of ascent.

Multi-stage rise: This is for experienced fliers in conditions of a good wind. In this technique, the kite rises by stages: after launch, pull at the line, and the kite will rise to a certain altitude as a result of the increased speed of the kite relative to the frontal wind and the consequent increase of the lift on the kite; slowly let out line and the kite will slightly lose altitude but not too much; then give the line another pull to make the kite rise to a new altitude. Keep repeating this operation until the kite climbs to the desired altitude. This is a popular way of flying a kite among the Chinese populace.

FIG. 104   *Crab* by Liu Bin
Soft-wing kite
This is a crab kite with its eight legs spreading horizontally.

Flight Control

For various reasons a kite may bank left or right during its ascent. When this happens you need to immediately correct the problem by pulling the line in the opposite direction. If the kite leans at a steep angle and pulling the line fails to correct the problem, you should immediately release the line to allow the kite to right itself as it floats downward, then tighten your grip on the line to make it rise again.

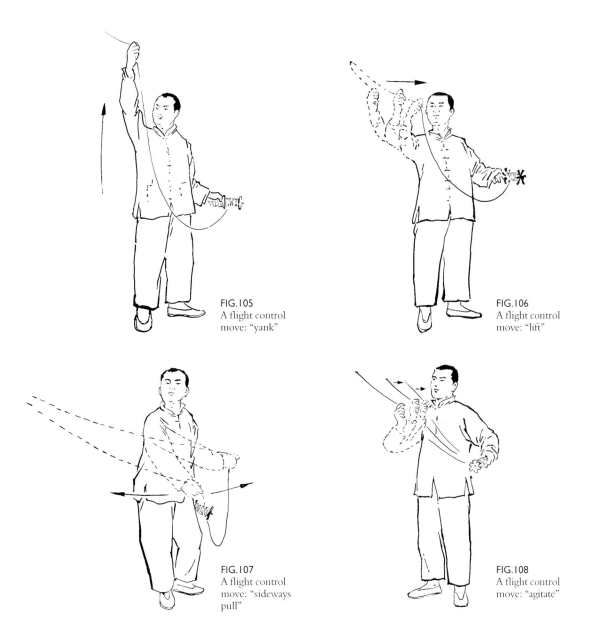

FIG.105
A flight control
move: "yank"

FIG.106
A flight control
move: "lift"

FIG.107
A flight control
move: "sideways
pull"

FIG.108
A flight control
move: "agitate"

Generations of Chinese kite fliers have come up with the four following flight control moves:

"Yank" (FIG. 105): when the kite leans on its side, raise the hand holding the flying line and yank it backwards to increase lift.

"Lift" (FIG. 106): when the kite sinks, "yank" and tug at the line and at the same time lift the line upwards.

"Sideways pull" (FIG. 107): when the kite sways to the left, pull the line to the left so that the right wing will take more wind and the left wing can right itself. Do the same for swaying to the right.

"Agitate" (FIG. 108): agitate the line to increase wind lift so that the kite rises and stabilizes.

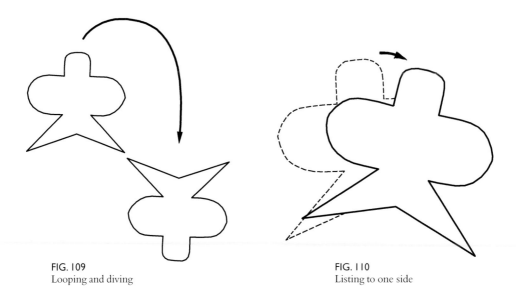

FIG. 109
Looping and diving

FIG. 110
Listing to one side

3. Common Problems and How to Adjust for Them

The first time a new kite is flown, problems are expected and they usually can be fixed. Kites that are flown after having been left in storage for some time can also run into problems because of warping, wear and damage. They need to be fixed too. Fixing flight problems is an important job after the manufacture of a kite. To fix them, you need to observe and analyze it in flight, make adjustments and conduct tests. How well you make adjustments to correct the flight problems depends on your experience in kite flying and on your grasp of flight aerodynamics.

Flight problems can be grouped into six categories. Sometimes the problems encountered by a kite can fall into more than one category and they need to be tackled one by one after the causes are determined. It may happen that after several attempts at adjustments, problems remain unsolved. In this case you need to revisit the problem to find out if your judgment was correct. If your judgment proves correct, then you will need to look for causes in the kite design. We will not however discuss kite design problems here. The following are six typical problems encountered when flying a kite and we show how they can be fixed.

Looping and Diving

A kite in flight suddenly turning upside down and diving to the ground (FIG. 109).

Adjustments you can make:

A. Add a weight to the tail section of the kite to shift the center of gravity toward the tail.

B. Bend the tail section toward the back of the kite.

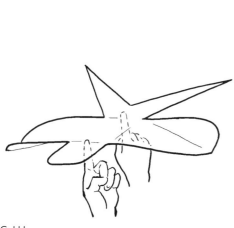

FIG. 111
With the central spar supported on one hand, check for any left-right imbalance.

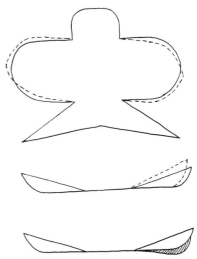

FIG. 112
Check for any shape asymmetry between left and right.

C. Move the bridle line slightly forward.

Make incremental adjustments. Test after each small adjustment and observe the flight to decide on further adjustments.

Listing to One Side

A kite unable to maintain an upright position and tending to lean to one side (FIG. 110).

Adjustments you can make:

A. With the kite's central spar supported on one hand, observe if there is left-right balance. If you find the kite is heavier on one side and leans to that side, then it's possible that the listing is caused by this uneven distribution of weight. To fix the problem, try adding a weight to the lighter side (FIG. 111).

B. Check for shape asymmetry. Left-right asymmetry in area, frame construction and rigidity can cause imbalance in uneven distribution of the wind force which in turn causes the kite to list to one side (FIG. 112).

Tip: Weight Imbalance VS Uneven Distribution of Wind Force

Kites have some degree of inherent transverse stability and are normally not affected by slight weight imbalances. Other factors (such as lopsided warping of the kite) could result in uneven distribution of wind force on the kite and affect the flight of a kite.

If the heavier side of the kite turns out to be the upside of the tilt in flight, the listing clearly is not caused by weight imbalance but rather by uneven distribution of wind force from other causes, such as air turbulences or bridle line imbalance.

If it is a hard-wing kite, make sure the two wings are of identical size; in the case of a soft-wing kite, make sure the wing pockets generated by the wind on the two wings are of equal size. Correct any asymmetry.

C. Adjust the bridle lines. Shift the main bridle line (i.e. the tow point) toward the side of tilting. Determine the amount of shift by test flying.

Swaying

Swaying differs from listing in that the kite swings alternately to the left and the right and ends up dropping to the ground (FIG. 113). Rocking could also be a problem in flight.

Adjustments you can make:

A. Shift the main bridle line downward, but not by much, otherwise other problems could ensue. Test as you adjust, as appropriate. If there are several bridle lines, widening the distances between the lines may help.

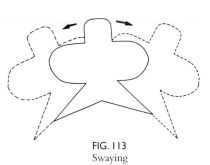

FIG. 113
Swaying

B. Kites with a single bridle line are more prone to rocking. To correct it, you can add a line along the central spar. Rocking is not always a bad thing. Some kites (such as small swallow kites) are meant to rock to impart an impression of a bird weaving through the air.

Forward Pitch

This is the phenomenon of a kite pitching forward whenever the flying line is pulled (FIG. 114). In the case of a kite with a single bridle line, you can shift the tow point downward. If there are two or three bridle lines, you can try shortening the lengths of the lines and shift the main bridle line downward to increase the kite's ability to lift its front end.

Forward pitching can be any of the following situations:

A. Whenever you tighten the grip on the line, the kite pitches forward and as soon as the grip is loosened, the kite rights itself and rears its head in the course of the downward drift; when you tug at the line again, the kite pitches forward anew. This is a sign that the position of the bridle lines is too forward and you can correct the problem by shifting the tow point backward.

B. Once the kite starts to pitch forward, the problem persists and the kite is unable to right itself. It can be caused either by a design flaw or, more likely, the center of gravity

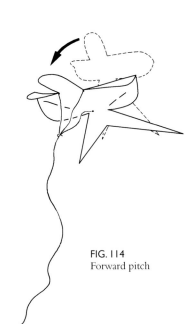

FIG. 114
Forward pitch

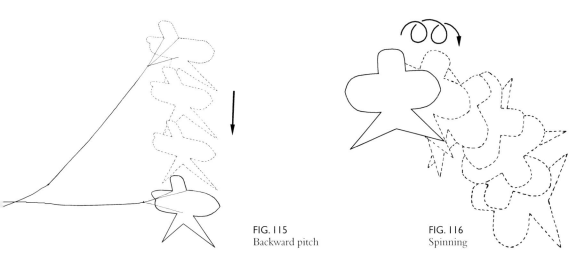

FIG. 115
Backward pitch

FIG. 116
Spinning

being too forward. To correct the problem, you can add an appropriate weight to the tail section and also shift the bridle line toward the tail.

C. The kite flies normally in the beginning, but starts to pitch forward when a certain altitude is reached; when the line is loosened, the kite does not keep pitching and dropping to the ground but instead continues to glide in the air. This is a common occurrence with soft-wing eagle kites; the problem can be addressed by quickly winding in the line. No other adjustments are necessary.

Backward Pitch

This happens when the kite has a hard time gaining altitude, although the wind pulls it taut; the kite may go out a long way but not rise high enough, so that the flying line forms a very small angle with the ground; when the wind falls, the kite falls in a "lean back" posture (FIG. 115).

Adjustments you can make:

A. Shift the bridle lines forward. If there are more than one bridle lines, make the anterior line shorter and the posterior line longer.

B. Heavier kites are more prone to run into this problem. Try reducing the weight of the tail section.

Spinning

Fast spinning of the kite to the left or the right (FIG. 116).

This could have many causes and can be corrected only after repeated testing:

A. In a kite with a single bridle line, the tow point may not be properly positioned crosswise and this could result in an uneven distribution of wind force and consequently spinning.

B. Imbalance in the tying of multiple bridle lines may cause spinning also.

C. Warping of the kite caused by the force of the wind could also result in spinning.

D. It is not uncommon for kites with too small a lateral area to run into the problem of spinning.

FIG. 117 *Cicada* by Liu Bin
Paddle Kite
In Chinese culture, cicada is regarded as a sacred insect. The wings are of
diaphanous nature.

APPENDICES

Common Designs Featured on Chinese Kites

Common designs featured on Chinese kites are mostly drawn from China's age-old culture of auspicious symbols. These auspicious patterns fraught with meanings express popular hopes and good wishes.

Pattern and Design	Name and Description
	Bat Bat (*fu*, 蝠), homophonous to good fortune (*fu*, 福), symbolizes good luck and happiness. Bat patterns come in a variety of postures and are amenable to insertion in different parts of the painted sail of a kite. It can be combined with peaches, which symbolize longevity, to form *fu shou*, meaning "good luck and longevity" or with a pattern of "coin with an eye in the middle" (*tong qian*) to give *fu zai yan qian*, meaning "good luck right in front your eyes".
	Butterfly Butterfly (*hu die*), whose second character is homophonous to octogenarian (*die*), symbolizes longevity. Due to its bright colors and the beautiful patterns on its wings, the butterfly is often combined with flowers to suggest romantic love and a happy marriage. Butterfly patterns can be added to a painted sail as an ornamental element as well as serve as the main theme of a kite.

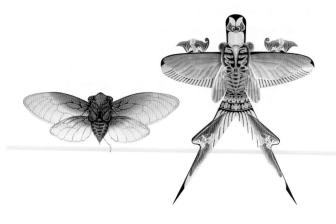

Cicada

Cicada (*chan*) can mean succession (*chan lian*) in Chinese and therefore symbolizes continuity, an unbroken run of good luck. The cicada's habitat high in the tree tops and its supposed ability to survive on dew only give it an added symbolic meaning of noble character. Cicadas can be added to a painted sail as an ornamental element or serve as the main theme of a kite.

Cloud

The cloud pattern is a typically Chinese auspicious pattern. It suggests a romantic carefree spirit; it is an intricate pattern with a sense of motion and variety, and symbolizes good luck and fulfilment of one's wishes.

Dragon

Dragons are credited with magic powers in legend and symbolize imperial authority. Dragons can be added to a painted sail as an ornamental element as well as serve as the main theme of the kite.

Pattern and Design	Name and Description

Fish

Fish (*yu*, 鱼), homophonous to surplus (*yu*, 余), symbolizes wealth, a cornucopia of riches. Fish can be added to the painted sail of a kite as an ornamental element or serve on its own as the main theme of the painted sail.

Gourd

Gourd (*hu lu*), which sounds like good fortune and prosperity (*fu lu*), symbolizes happiness and wealth and stature. The multitude of seeds in a gourd also make it a symbol of "plenty of male heirs", which is counted as one of the greatest blessings in traditional China.

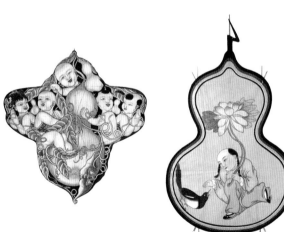

Pattern and Design	Name and Description

Lotus Flower

Lotus (*he*), homophonous to harmony (*he*), symbolizes harmony and happiness; the lotus is also a symbol of purity in Buddhism.

Peach

According to mythology, the immortals offer their guests peaches, which have come to be associated with longevity.

Peony

The peony, one of the ten most highly valued flowers in China, boasts a complex arrangement of petals and gorgeous colors. It symbolizes wealth and elegance in Chinese culture.

Pattern and Design	Name and Description

Perforated Coin

Coin or money (*qian*), homophonous to "in front" (*qian*), is often combined with a bat pattern, with the "coin with an eye" painted in front of the bat's eyes, to suggest "bat or good fortune" (*fu*) is right in front of your eyes.

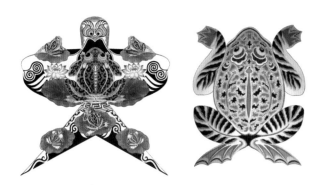

Toad

Toad (*chan chu*), with the first character homophonous to cicada, is often combined with the water-lily (*lian* in Chinese) patterns to give *chan lian*, meaning an unbroken succession and continuity.

Water Lily

The water-lily with its beautiful flowers symbolizes good luck and happiness.

Bibliography

1. Wang Hongxun, Xu Shuyan, *zhongguo fengzheng* [Chinese Kites]. Heilongjiang: Heilongjiang chubanshe (Heilongjiang Fine Arts Publishing House), 1994

2. Fei Baoling, *cao xueqin zhayan fengzheng tupu kaogong zhi* [A Technical and Pictorial Compilation Detailing Kite Making in the Cao Xueqin Tradition). Taiwan: hansheng zazhishe (Han Sheng Magazine Publishing Co.), 1998

3. Wang Qinian, Wu Guanghui, Yu Jiming, *fengzheng* [Kites]. Beijing: renmin tiyu chubanshe (People's Sports Publishing House), 1986

4. Kong Xiangze, Kong Lingmin, Kong Bingzhang, *cao xueqin fengzheng yishu* [The Art of Cao Xueqin's Kites]. Beijing: Beijing gongyi meishu chubanshe (Beijing Arts and Crafts Publishing House), 2004

5. Ha Kuiming, Ha Yiqi, *zhongguo hashi fengzheng* [Ha-Styel Chinese Kites]. Hong Kong: shangwu yinshuguan xianggang fenguan (Commercial Press, Hong Kong), 1986

6. Feng Jicai, *minjian fengzheng* [Folk Kites]. Hebei: Hebei shaonian ertong chubanshe (Hebei Children's Publishing House), 2004

FIG. 118 *The Monkey King Thrice Beats the White Bone Spirit* by Liu Bin
Hard-wing kite
The theme is taken from the famous novel *Journey to the West*. A typical Beijing kite, it is different from Weifang kite, despite the same theme (see FIG. 67 on page 40).

Dates of the Chinese Dynasties

Xia Dynasty（夏）..2070–1600 BC

Shang Dynasty（商）..1600–1046 BC

Zhou Dynasty（周）...1046–256 BC

    Western Zhou Dynasty（西周）.....................................1046–771 BC

    Eastern Zhou Dynasty（东周）.....................................770–256 BC

      Spring and Autumn Period（春秋）...........................770–476 BC

      Warring States Period（战国）.................................475–221 BC

Qin Dynasty（秦）...221–206 BC

Han Dynasty（汉）...206 BC–220 AD

    Western Han Dynasty（西汉）......................................206 BC–25 AD

    Eastern Han Dynasty（东汉）......................................25–220

Three Kingdoms（三国）...220–280

    Wei（魏）..220–265

    Shu Han（蜀）...221–263

    Wu（吴）...222–280

Jin Dynasty（晋）..265–420

    Western Jin Dynasty（西晋）.......................................265–316

    Eastern Jin Dynasty（东晋）.......................................317–420

Northern and Southern Dynasties（南北朝）...............................420–589

    Southern Dynasties（南朝）...420–589

    Liang Dynasty（梁）...502–557

    Northern Dynasties（北朝）...439–581

Sui Dynasty（隋）..581–618

Tang Dynasty（唐）...618–907

Five Dynasties and Ten Kingdoms（五代十国）...........................907–960

    Five Dynasties（五代）..907–960

    Ten Kingdoms（十国）...902–979

Song Dynasty（宋）...960–1279

    Northern Song Dynasty（北宋）....................................960–1127

    Southern Song Dynasty（南宋）....................................1127–1279

Liao Dynasty（辽）..916–1125

Jin Dynasty（金）..1115–1234

Xixia Dynasty (or Tangut)（西夏）...1038–1227

Yuan Dynasty（元）...1279–1368

Ming Dynasty（明）...1368–1644

Qing Dynasty（清）...1644–1911

Index

scraping 46, 60, 63, 66, 67, 111, 117

seagull 78

secondary spar (of frame) 115, 116, 117, 121

second-tier wing edge (of frame) 109, 111, 113

shaving 46, 48, 60, 62, 63, 66, 67, 69, 111

shear lashing(s) 68, 69, 71, 79, 91, 92, 101, 104, 109, 111, 115, 117, 123, 124

sifter kite 20

single-string connection (of tying) 77, 85

skin (of bamboo) 43, 44, 45, 60, 61, 63, 64, 79, 102, 103

slit-end (of attachment) 68, 92, 96, 104, 124

soft-wing kite 4, 14, 15, 17, 22, 23, 24, 29, 30, 31, 34, 35, 36, 37, 40, 50, 54, 74, 78, 81, 100, 108, 133, 136, 140, 141
   multiple-layer soft-wing 17, 108
   single-layer soft-wing 17
   soft-wing (compound) 30, 40, 54

spider 20

splicing (of attachment) 68, 69

splitting 45, 46, 60, 61, 62, 66
   basic split 61
   fingernail split 61
   pierce split 61
   wiggle split 61

strip (of bamboo) 16, 17, 18, 19, 29, 33, 34, 36, 43, 44, 45, 46, 48, 54, 59, 60, 61, 62, 63,

64, 66, 68, 69, 70, 71, 83, 92, 94, 95, 98, 99, 101, 115, 117

Sun Wen 36

swastika (pattern) 29

symmetrical splitting 66, 87, 91, 110, 111, 116, 123

T

tail section (of frame) 15, **27**, 29, 37, 39, 79, 104, 138, 141

tail spar (of frame) 101, 103, 104, 105, 123, 124, 126

tail streamer 15, 82, 84, 85, 90, 93

Tang Jinkun 12, 30, 40, 50

temple-variety (style) 12

three-string connection (of tying) 77, 89

Tianjin kite 30, 41

tiger 39, 58

toad 27, 147

treasure bowl 40

trimming 62, 63, 64, 75, 101, 106

turnip 4, 32

Two Immortals of Harmony and Unity 16

two-string connection (of tying) 77, 93, 99, 113

U

upper wing edge (of frame) 115, 116, 118, 123, 124

V

vine 39, 81

W

waist section 6, 25, 28, 29

water lily 27, 147

Wei Yuantai 41

Weifang kite 31, 41

wild goose 4, 24

wing load 131, 133, 135

wing loop (of frame) 79, 101, 102, 104, 105

wing pocket 117, 118, 120, 124, 140

woodblock picture (print) 30, 31, 41

Workshop of the Qing dynasty imperial household 11

Wulin Reminiscences (Wu Lin Jiu Shi) 35

X

Xie Zongke 35

Xu Wei 36

Y

Yang Tongke (kite-maker) 31

Yang Zhou Hua Fang Lu 37

yellow inner layer (of pulp) 43, 44

yin-yang (diagram) 97

Z

Zhao Xin 33

Zhao Yushan 39

Zhi Ruili (kite-maker) 4, 17, 21, 23, 25, 27, 128

Zhou Mi 35

Zhou Shutang (kite-maker) 30, 40, 54